Almost Home

Stories of Hope
and the Human Spirit
in the Neonatal ICU

CHRISTINE GLEASON

© 2009 Christine Gleason.

Published by Kaplan Publishing, a division of Kaplan, Inc.
1 Liberty Plaza, 24th Floor
New York, NY 10006

Printed in the United States of America

9 8 7 6 5 4 3 2 1

Library of Congress Cataloging-in-Publication Data

Gleason, Christine A.
Almost home : stories of hope and the human spirit in the neonatal ICU / Christine Gleason.
       p. cm.
   ISBN 978-1-60714-049-8
1. Gleason, Christine A. 2. Neonatologists--United States--Biography.
3. Neonatal intensive care. I. Title.
   RJ253.5.G54 2009
   618.92'01--dc22

                                        2008041277

Kaplan Publishing books are available at special quantity discounts to use for sales promotions, employee premiums, or educational purposes. Please email our Special Sales Department to order or for more information at kaplanpublishing@kaplan.com, or write to Kaplan Publishing, 1 Liberty Plaza, 24th Floor, New York, NY 10006.

DEDICATION

To Erik, who has shown me
that love really can last a life-time

And to Kristen, Lauren and Erin—
my very own beloved babies

CONTENTS

AN INVITATION vii

CHAPTER 1 *Jimmy* 1

CHAPTER 2 *Owen* 15

CHAPTER 3 *Jazmine* 23

CHAPTER 4 *Linda* 39

CHAPTER 5 *Patrick* 47

CHAPTER 6 *Hannah* 59

CHAPTER 7 *Roxie* 69

CHAPTER 8 *Emily* 85

CHAPTER 9 *Travis* 97

CHAPTER 10 *Joshua* 117

CHAPTER 11 *Christopher* 133

CHAPTER 12 *Erica* 151

CHAPTER 13 *Anna* 167

CHAPTER 14 *Harry* 185

CHAPTER 15 *Baby X* 209

EPILOGUE *Mitchell and Michael* 223

ACKNOWLEDGEMENTS 245

I SAT AT THE top of the wide staircase in the middle of a large, noisy lobby filled with children of various ages and their parents. On each knee I held a squirming four-year-old boy; identical twin brothers born just six months into their mother's pregnancy, at birth the boys had weighed a little over one pound each. Below me on the staircase sat at least another dozen sets of twins, three sets of triplets, one set of quadruplets, and one trio that was missing a quadruplet sibling who hadn't made it. They were all graduates of the hospital's Neonatal Intensive Care Unit, or NICU. Some had stayed for just a few days, many for weeks, and some for months. The occasion was the hospital's annual NICU Grad Party, an opportunity for parents to show off their offspring and to reconnect with the hospital staff who had cared for them during their children's dark early days. It was also a chance for the hospital staff to rejoice in the results of their considerable efforts and to find out how their tiny patients did once they left the hospital.

As we posed for the annual "multiples" picture, I hugged Bobby and Sammy a little tighter. They were so warm, so alive, but I was pretty sure they wouldn't have been in my lap that day if they'd been born just one year earlier than they had. They'd been among the first babies at the hospital to receive liquid surfactant into their lungs, a new treatment for a premature lung disease that accounted for most of the deaths in the NICU, including that of Patrick

Bouvier Kennedy, President John F. Kennedy's premature baby boy, in 1963. We were all astonished when Bobby and Sammy, born at just 24 weeks' gestation and white males to boot (who usually had the worst lung disease), were on ventilators for only one week and didn't have the usual laundry list of preemie complications. Without severe lung disease to contend with, they could handle the immaturity of their other organs more easily.

After the multiples picture was taken, I stepped up to the microphone at a podium that had been positioned at the base of the stairs. As medical director of the NICU, it was time for me to give my annual welcome speech. I unfolded the piece of paper that Linda, the NICU social worker, had handed me that morning. She had jotted down a few remarkable names and numbers from the RSVP list for me to read to the waiting crowd—including the tiniest baby (birth weight 1 pound 2 ounces), the longest NICU stay (17 months), the biggest baby (birth weight 12 pounds 6 ounces), and the oldest baby present. That was an 18-year-old high school student who reluctantly came up to the podium and shook my hand as I announced to the cheering crowd that this now 230-pound linebacker for his school football team was once a two-pound preemie in our NICU.

When I'd finished my speech, I left the podium and plunged into the noisy throng, recognizing the parents of several babies I had cared for over the years.

"Dr. Gleason!" they'd exclaim. "Over here! Look at Jamie now. Can you believe she was once so small, and so sick?"

We'd hug and I'd admire their little whirling dervish, or their sulking adolescent, and perhaps pose for another picture or two. I've kept all those pictures, some of which matched pictures I'd saved of the same baby in the NICU or of me holding the baby on home-going day. Parents usually expressed, each in his or her own way, their heartfelt gratitude for the care that their children, and they themselves, had received. They often shared with me their considerable relief that the experience was over and they could get on with their lives and the raising of their children. I drank it all in, savoring these conversations and the sight of all these happy, healthy kids who at one time had been so tiny and so sick, lying in incubators in the NICU, hooked up to all sorts of intensive care equipment and with no certainty that they were going to survive.

This book is a collection of stories about children—babies, mostly—whom I have known and cared for during my career as a neonatologist, a doctor who specializes in the care of newborn infants. Most of the stories take place in the NICU, a strange and wonderful place where both miracles and tragedies happen every day. I'd like to invite you to take a deep breath and step into that place with me. If you're like most people, you've never been inside one except perhaps to visit a friend's or relative's premature baby. You probably think that it must be a terribly difficult place to work and at times it is, especially when a baby dies. But the NICU is really a very hopeful place, a fact that is evident at those NICU grad parties. Most of the babies who begin their lives there survive, go home with their parents, and do well.

These are the stories that have moved me the most and simply needed to be told. The events I've described are true, although in most cases I have changed real names, settings, and other identifiers to protect privacy. Some of the stories are unbearably sad. I cried when they happened, I cried as I wrote them, and I cry every time I reread them. Others tell of babies who survived and did well, against seemingly impossible odds. And a few of the stories are downright embarrassing, especially those that chronicle my tentative early years as a doctor-in-training.

My hope is that together with me, you, the reader of these stories, will celebrate the miracles of modern medicine, mourn its failings, and marvel at the strength of the human spirit, so evident in these children and their families, and in the dedicated people who staff the NICU.

CHAPTER I

Jimmy

As I stepped off the elevator on the sixth floor of Rainbow Babies and Children's Hospital, I felt my heart squeeze and my hands chill. I was terrified. What did I know about taking care of sick newborn babies? It was September 1979, the third month of my pediatric internship. I had spent the first two months in the emergency room, where I generally saw otherwise healthy kids who had ear infections, sore throats, broken bones, and stomachaches. Actually, I felt as though I was getting pretty good at my job there. Even in the "real" emergencies, I was beginning to feel like part of the team. But this was different. Here in the Neonatal Intensive Care Unit, everything would be a real emergency, at least potentially. I tried to think reassuring thoughts, but I was nearly paralyzed by fear. Finally, I was jolted from my misery by the senior resident, who saw me heading slowly toward the entrance to the NICU.

"Morning rounds begin at 7:30, Chris, and it's a *ZOO* in there, so move it. You've inherited 10 babies from the last intern and a couple of them are *REAL SICK.*"

My terror intensified to speechless inertia, but I managed to walk onto the unit and dump my coat and bag in the residents' room, a room that normally looked as if a cyclone had hit it. As I looked down the hall, I could see the other two interns, the senior resident, and the head nurse already beginning rounds in the room directly opposite the nurses' station. This room contained eight incubators, and in those incubators were, I discovered, the unit's most desperately ill babies. I had inherited four of them.

Rounds had begun on someone else's baby, a full-term newborn who looked enormous, even to me. After I was briefly introduced to everyone, I received my first dose of nursery lingo. This huge baby was an LGA IDM with HMD, LVH, and a possible IVH. Having little idea what this all meant, I listened for clues during the discussion and gathered that she was large for gestational age (LGA) because she was an infant of a diabetic mother (IDM) and because of this, her lungs were immature (hyaline membrane disease, HMD), her heart was enlarged (left ventricular hypertrophy, LVH), and she might have developed brain bleeding (intraventricular hemorrhage, IVH). While I was inwardly sighing with relief that this complex but treatable disaster wasn't mine, we moved on to the next incubator, where the tiniest baby I had ever seen was lying on his back, attached to what seemed like miles of tubes and wires.

"This is one of yours, Chris," yawned Greg, the senior resident, "and good luck; this kid's been here for three weeks and hasn't made any progress."

As I tried to assume an air of professional detached appraisal, I saw the baby open his eyes and for an instant, he seemed to look directly at me. Leo Sayer was at that moment singing "Sad eyes, turn the other way, I don't want to see you cry" on the room's radio, and all I could think of was what sad eyes *this* baby had. Apparently, he had been born at 24 weeks' gestation, which was the legal limit for an abortion in many states at that time. Greg was filling me in on his extensive list of problems, except that he kept referring to the baby as *she*.

"She's had every complication of prematurity you can think of" (this was quite limited in my case)—"HMD, BPD, IVH, PDA, NEC, and of course As and Bs" (of course!). "Now she's dependent on the respirator and she just won't grow." This meant that his lungs were immature and badly damaged; he'd had a brain hemorrhage; a blood vessel leading from his heart to his lungs hadn't closed normally; his bowels had become inflamed and he'd had bloody stools; and he regularly forgot to breathe (apnea), causing his heart rate to slow down (bradycardia).

It seemed sort of silly but I just had to ask, "Isn't this a baby *boy*?"

"Oh, yeah…Baby Boy Jackson. Well, it really doesn't make much difference; it's usually only the parents who really care and we never see this one's mother—she's only 15, still in high school, and she never even realized she was pregnant. Anyway, Jackson needs a blood transfusion today, and she needs blood drawn every four hours to make sure her ventilator settings are correct." I began to realize that sexual ambiguity was one shield that residents used to keep themselves emotionally detached.

Morning rounds were finally over and it seemed to me that I had mountains of crucial tasks to perform. I was to learn later that no staff members were ever finished with their work on this unit. The key to success was to establish priorities so that the truly important things got done and the others simply waited for another time. But I didn't know that then. I looked at my list of patients and my checklist of things to do and I felt sick inside. One of my fellow interns must have noticed, because he came over and asked if I was going to the blood bank to get blood for Jackson.

"Well," I said, "actually, I have no idea where it is or what to do when I get there or even what's involved in getting a baby transfused." He began to explain the initial process to me but was interrupted by a stat page to the delivery room. We were on call for high-risk deliveries every third day and night, and today was his turn. I would get mine tomorrow. So right now, I was alone again in my tasks. Everyone else was busy, but at least they all seemed to know what they were doing. Somehow I managed to fill out the appropriate forms and to call the blood bank to order the blood. One of the nurses was watching me and when I'd finished, she asked if I had gotten the type and cross done on the baby. Again, I tried to adopt a professional air as I muttered, "Gee, one more order to write."

"No," she said, "you don't *order* a type and cross; you *draw* it."

This felt like a moment of truth. She watched me approach the baby's incubator with the blood-drawing equipment. Each incubator had two portholes facing the front, allowing parents and staff to reach in and handle the babies without letting in the relatively cold room air. Unfortunately, the portholes were closed and I had no idea how to open them. I glanced around the room and spotted a young mother expertly changing her premature baby's diaper inside the incubator. Casually, I approached her and started up a conversation, which I continued until she'd finished and had shut the portholes.

"Well, would you look at that!" I exclaimed. "There she goes again," and sure enough, that blessed little preemie had wet the tiny diaper her mother had just placed under her tiny bottom. I watched the mother push a button on each porthole as she pulled it toward her and then placed her hands inside the attached rubber sleeves.

I returned to Jackson's incubator and managed to get both my hands and the blood-drawing equipment inside. Now came the hardest part—drawing the blood. I knew that since the baby no longer had an umbilical artery catheter (which is very convenient for drawing blood), his blood would have to be obtained by "heel-stick." As I prepared the skin with alcohol, I glanced at the baby's face. He was staring intently at me, with his brow wrinkled and his eyes worried. He seemed to know what was coming as soon as the alcohol preparation was applied to his heel. I pricked his heel with the lance, and his eyes squeezed shut. When I'd finished, he turned his head away from me. He was so young, and yet his premature entry into the world had made him so old.

I spent the rest of the morning poring over charts, doing heel-sticks, writing orders, and gingerly examining each of my babies. It was hard to admit, but I was actually scared of them. Their medical problems seemed so overwhelming and they were so fragile. Early in the afternoon, as I became aware that I was already exhausted, the blood bank called and said that the blood was ready for Jackson. I went down and picked it up and handed it to his nurse. "Please transfuse 15 cc's over about four hours," I ordered. She looked me straight in the eye and said, "Blood may only be given by a physician." This was really too much. I had no idea how to get blood out of that bag and into the baby, and the nurse must have seen it done hundreds of times. She remained silent.

I picked up the bag and a blood filter (at least I knew *that* much) and some syringes and disappeared into the privacy of the "treatment room"—a separate room off the main infant ward that was devoted primarily to procedures. There, I proceeded to impale the bag with the filter. So far, so good. As I assembled the syringes, I was feeling somewhat smug. I would figure this out. After all, I *was* a doctor.

I hung the bag up on the intravenous pole but as I turned to pick up the syringes, I heard a sudden *whuump* and then the unmistakable sound of liquid hitting the floor at high speed. The filter had popped out, and blood was gushing from the hole I'd made in the bag. I grabbed the bag and inverted it in time to save some of the blood. Then the door opened. It was the chief resident, and there I was, holding onto that bloody bag. And there was blood all over me, the floor, and nearly everything else, it seemed. I could feel tears welling up in my eyes.

He silently put on a pair of rubber gloves, fixed the bag somehow, and expertly filled several syringes with blood. As I washed my hands and wiped up the floor and countertops, he said, "Trust me, it *will* get better." Then he handed me the filled and capped syringes and walked out of the room. Somehow baby Jackson received his blood transfusion, and I muddled my way through the rest of my long "to do" list for the rest of the day, and well into the night.

The chief resident was right, though. After that terrible first day, things slowly got better and, although I still felt insecure and overwhelmed, I began to manage the daily routine work more efficiently. I also began to realize that neonatal intensive care is tough to leave behind at the end of the day. One night I woke up my startled husband to let him know that there were several babies, in incubators and on ventilators, who were in our bathroom and who needed my care. It wasn't until I actually opened the bathroom door and turned on the light that I realized it had just been a dream. All "my" babies were being cared for in the hospital and were not my responsibility—at least not that night. It took me at least an hour to fall back to sleep, wondering how they were doing.

One day, as I was starting yet another new IV on baby Jackson and gazing again into his sad eyes, it occurred to me that neither I nor anyone else had seen or spoken with his mother. And another thing occurred to me: He still had no first name. Some parents avoided naming their babies until they were out of the woods. A mother once confided to me that she was afraid she'd have to "bury the family name." But although Jackson was still on a respirator, he was now four weeks old, and had passed the most critical period. I guessed that he now had a slightly better than 50/50 chance to make it.

When I'd finished putting in his IV (for yet another blood transfusion), I walked down to the social worker's office and found

Sally Wainwright. She looked harassed and irritable. I asked her about Jackson's family, and she sighed in response to my questions. "You'd better leave that one alone, Chris. His mother is a 15-year-old high school dropout. She lives about 100 miles from here in a trailer park. She has enough to worry about, and she really doesn't want to get involved."

"Has anyone *asked* her about that lately?" I wondered. "I mean, maybe it's more trouble for us to try and get her involved, but wouldn't she *have* to be involved if he makes it home some day?"

"Forget about that touchy-feely bonding stuff in this case, Chris. You'd really be wasting your time. Believe me, she wants nothing to do with him. She may even give him up for adoption or perhaps he'll be placed in foster care, if he lives."

I just didn't want to believe Sally, and so I decided to find out for myself. My first obstacle was the mother's phone number. She hadn't given us one. When Sally confirmed this, I realized that no one had been able to speak to her since she'd been discharged from the hospital—three days after the baby's birth. I thought she must be imagining all sorts of things about her baby. Something needed to be done, and I decided that I was the one to do it.

I began my search one night when I was on call. I spoke with directory assistance in the girl's small Ohio town and located several people with the last name Jackson. I hoped that one of them would turn out to be a relative. Amazingly, on my second try, I located her older sister. After I carefully explained who I was, she told me that Karen Jackson lived in a trailer with her boyfriend, but that she often visited their mother, who lived down the street—and had a telephone. After several entreaties to the baby's "auntie," she finally gave me that number, but it was two days later before I had a chance to use it. A big, beautiful newborn baby had suddenly become very sick and was transferred from the regular nursery to us. She was dead within 48 hours, and we were all baffled. She had developed pneumonia and then her heart had become inflamed, and we didn't know why. Only later did we receive the autopsy results: overwhelming Coxsackie B viral infection. These infections are usually benign in older kids, but in infants they can be fatal, and there's no specific treatment. Somehow, knowing the diagnosis didn't help us much. We all felt terribly defeated. This baby wasn't like one of our preemies. She looked like one of those babies in the Gerber baby-food ads.

The next morning, I pulled out the piece of paper with Karen Jackson's mother's number from my white coat pocket and dialed it. A weary-sounding older woman answered on the sixth ring. I identified myself, and immediately I sensed hostility in her voice.

"Karen never asks about the baby," she told me. "And I'm just as glad. She should give it up for adoption if it lives. I don't want her making any silly attachments now which would be hard to break later." I told her that I sympathized with her but that I was the baby's advocate now. And he was getting better, but still had no name and he needed his mother.

Her voice softened a bit as she whispered, "Is he really getting better? How much does he weigh now?"

When I told her, she sighed, "Jackson boys have always been fighters." I explained that I simply wanted to give Karen a progress report. I knew that even if she didn't ask about her baby, she still had to be wondering. Her mother said she might come over the next morning and I could try then. But she suspected that no good would come of it, no good at all. I called the next morning and three successive mornings, but there was no answer. I felt duped—and naïve and inexperienced. But I persisted, and on the fifth morning, the phone was finally answered by Karen's mother. She told me that Karen was there but she warned me to remember what she'd told me. I promised her that I would be careful.

Then, a very young voice came on the phone and said, "So

you're the doctor taking care of him. Why are you calling me now?" I proceeded to give her the baby's progress report, noting the improvements he'd made on the respirator, the fact that he was tolerating small amounts of formula by feeding tube and was starting to gain weight. She expressed little interest in any of this until, at the very end of my spiel, I mentioned how alert he was, and how his eyes always seemed to be following me during any procedures or exams.

"His eyes are sad sometimes," I explained, "but they're also curious."

She was surprised. "You mean, he opens his eyes and *looks* at you? When I saw him in the delivery room, he was a bald, ugly red thing and I couldn't even see where his eyes were supposed to be."

I was encouraged by this burst of interest, so I went on to tell her that now he had a few wisps of red hair growing on the top of his head. I asked her if anyone else in the family had red hair.

"Uncle Jim does!" she shrieked. "Gee, red hair. I can't believe it." She said she had to leave for school soon, but I told her I could call again anytime to fill her in. She hesitated, but then we decided on Tuesday and Thursday mornings. At the last minute, I urged her to think of a name for the baby.

Over the next two weeks, I developed a telephone relationship with Karen Jackson. We'd spend most of our time talking about the little things—his hair, his eyes, how much he weighed, how much he was eating. One day a hospital volunteer brought in some little blue and pink knitted sweaters for all the babies. I put one on Baby Jackson and took a Polaroid picture and sent it to Karen. She was thrilled. "He *does* look just like Uncle Jim!" That was the day she finally named him.

He became Jimmy Jackson, and now we could all call him by his first name on rounds, instead of just Jackson. It seemed to me that a name earned him a bit more respect from the unit staff.

He had acquired both a name and a somewhat engaged parent. Unfortunately, though, respect was not a particularly good medicine for Jimmy. He wasn't doing very well. He'd stopped making improvements on the respirator; in fact, he was slipping. He'd also developed a heart murmur that sounded like a patent ductus arteriosus (PDA)—a normal blood vessel in fetuses, but one that causes trouble if it remains open after birth. PDAs often required surgical closure in preemies. I knew the surgery might help his lungs, but Jimmy seemed so small and fragile. He could die on the operating table. Over the next few days, we tried other ways to close his PDA but none worked, and he was definitely getting worse. I kept Karen abreast of these new developments, and my heart ached for her as I heard despair begin to creep into her young voice.

"Do you think he's going to die?" she whispered to me one day.

I tried to reassure her, telling her that he was strong and had proven himself to be a real fighter several times in the past few weeks.

"Like all the Jackson men," she said softly.

Jimmy finally went to the operating room early one morning and had his PDA closed. Karen had given her permission (although only 15 herself, as a mother, and an "emancipated minor," she could give legal consent). She was waiting by the phone at her mother's home for my call.

"He did beautifully," I told her, and I shared her relief.

He improved considerably over the next few days and we finally started making some progress on his ventilator settings. He began gaining real weight again (PDAs tend to make babies gain water weight). Karen and her mother made plans to take the bus to Cleveland for her first real visit with Jimmy and I helped them make the arrangements. I felt as though I had done the right thing, for both Jimmy *and* Karen.

But then he crashed. Overnight, Jimmy became desperately ill. His color turned gray; his surgical incision looked awful; and we had to turn his ventilator settings as high as they could go for a baby his size. Everyone agreed on the likely diagnosis: overwhelming sepsis, a toxic condition caused by the spread of bacteria in the blood. We started the most potent antibiotics we had and worked on getting his blood pressure back up, then waited to see if he'd respond. But he only got worse. He stopped moving and began bleeding from everywhere. His eyes went beyond sadness. The blood culture results came back and confirmed our worst fears — *Staphylococcus aureus* sepsis. There was nothing more we could do.

I had to call Karen, but how could I tell her this terrible news — that the baby boy she'd come to love and care about was going to die? I just had to steel myself for the worst and do it.

"Karen, this is Chris calling from the hospital. I'm so sorry to tell you this, but Jimmy has gotten really sick and I don't think he's going to make it." It was the worst telephone call I'd ever made. I urged her to come and be with Jimmy when he died; a baby needed his mother then, and a mother needed to be with her baby. She just sobbed and sobbed. Finally, her mother came on the line. Her voice was ice cold with anger.

"This is all your fault; you should have just let her be. Now she'll be miserable for the rest of her life. I wish we'd never talked to you, and we never want to speak to you again." I begged her to reconsider and reassured her that we would be here to help Karen through this, both now and after it was all over. She hung up on me. I sat there for a moment. Now I really questioned whether I'd done the right thing by getting Karen involved. Had I made a terrible mistake?

Jimmy had a very bad night and by morning, we all knew it was over. It was just a matter of time. His heart continued to beat only because he was attached to the respirator and powerful drugs were keeping it pumping, even though it had no power of its own. I called Karen again, but no one answered the phone.

We gave Jimmy some morphine and everyone agreed to try to keep him going until the afternoon, just in case his mother came. He needed a shot of "epi" (epinephrine, popularly known as adrenaline) at noon to keep his heart rate up, and we all knew time was running out. And then, at two o'clock, a teenage girl arrived in the NICU with her mother. I knew it was Karen. She had those same familiar sad eyes.

It was chaotic at first. We shut the doors to the NICU and someone wheeled over the "curtain of grief," as we called it—a privacy screen that was placed around Jimmy's incubator. Then, both Karen and her mother had their first real look at him. He looked awful now, but Karen just seemed to stare at his red hair and began sobbing inconsolably. I could see on the monitor that his heart rate was dropping quickly, so we brought over two rocking chairs and his bedside nurse and respiratory therapist managed to get Jimmy off the respirator and into his mother's arms. Suddenly it was quiet as Karen began rocking him slowly back and forth, stroking his tiny head and murmuring into his ear. I just stood nearby and silently sobbed. It was the most moving scene I'd ever witnessed. After a while, Karen passed Jimmy to her mother's arms and her mother held her grandson for the first and last time, her tears falling freely onto his head. Finally, I exchanged glances with Jimmy's nurse, who had gracefully and expertly arranged all this. I went over and listened to Jimmy's silent heart with my stethoscope, and I pronounced him dead. It was 3:19 P.M.

"He waited for you," I whispered to Karen.

We all retreated to the hall so Karen and her mother could be alone with Jimmy for a few minutes. Someone hurried past us, saw the screened-off incubator, and commented, "Staging another death scene?"

I felt drained. I had begun staging this so-called death scene a month ago, hadn't I? I was the one who'd finally gotten hold of

Karen and persuaded her to form an emotional bond with her baby. Had I really done her any favors?

The curtain moved aside, and Karen and her mother came out. They had put Jimmy back into his incubator, and the nurse went back in to make the final arrangements. Pictures would be taken; a lock of hair would be clipped and his footprints would be imprinted on a card.

Meanwhile, Karen signed some papers and Sally, the social worker, began helping the mother and daughter with preliminary funeral arrangements. And suddenly it was time for them to go. Karen looked so young and vulnerable to me, and I wanted to tell her how sorry I was about everything. But I just stood there. Then, she turned her sad, tear-stained face toward me and said, "For the first time, I really felt like his mother. He needed me and I was there for him. He was so beautiful, wasn't he?"

CHAPTER 2

Owen

My first night on call in the NICU was nearly my last. I had been dreading this night for months, knowing I alone would be responsible for all the sick babies in the unit, for 15 long hours. I would also be receiving any new admissions sent to the NICU from the newborn nursery, the labor and delivery suite, or from other area hospitals, by transport. I expected a cast of thousands.

At five o'clock, the entire NICU team assembled for "sign-out rounds," during which I frantically jotted down instructions from my departing colleagues on the care of their babies. Mostly, it was lab work. By the end of rounds, my "to do" list had 20 bilirubins, five post-transfusion hematocrits, 10 electrolyte levels, four complete blood counts, three chest X-rays to order and check, two blood transfusions, and a "septic workup." This last task called for obtaining blood, urine, and spinal fluid cultures from one of our preemies who had developed a fever during the afternoon. Cultures needed to be done before starting a baby on antibiotics to treat a possible infection. In those days, the hapless interns did all these tasks themselves. Today there are skilled nursing staff who perform nearly all these procedures, start intravenous lines, and

set up blood transfusions, but back then you were pretty much on
your own.

Eventually everyone left and I was finally alone with the nursing staff, and 30 sick babies. I went to work. First I made a prioritized "to do" list: what had to be done *now*, what had to be done
by morning rounds, and what could wait—perhaps indefinitely. I
started the septic workup first so that the baby could receive antibiotics soon after I was finished. The baby looked okay to me and
his temperature had gone down on its own. This was a good thing,
because it took me nearly an hour to get all the cultures done and
to start the IV for the antibiotics. Just as I was finishing up, my
beeper went off. It was the senior resident, telling me that my first
admission was on its way over from the newborn nursery. Apparently healthy at birth, the nurses had noticed that at about 24 hours
of age the baby was breathing too fast and wasn't interested in eating anymore. This could be a sign of many things, but I knew that
sepsis was one of the most ominous possibilities.

The senior resident confirmed that the baby needed a septic
workup and antibiotics—stat. He'd be bringing the baby over to
the treatment room, so I asked one of the nurses to help me with
the procedures and we started assembling the things we'd need.
The senior resident arrived a few minutes later with the baby in a
bassinet. In contrast to the preemie I'd just finished treating, this
baby looked very sick. He was pale and lethargic and in addition
to breathing faster than normal, he was making a kind of grunting
noise. The senior resident told me to get the cultures as fast as I
could; this baby really needed those antibiotics. I decided to start
with the spinal tap or lumbar puncture—a procedure used to obtain
a sample of spinal fluid in order to rule out meningitis. I'd done a
fair number of "LPs" while I was on my rotation in the emergency
room, so I felt more confident about getting it done than the other
procedures. But Murphy's Law applied (when something *can* go

wrong, it *will* go wrong); I just couldn't seem to get any spinal fluid from this baby.

The nurse held the baby in different positions while I tried different angles with the spinal needle, coming up dry each time. I was beginning to panic, and so was the nurse. This baby was getting sicker by the minute, not even crying or resisting any of our procedures. We decided to move ahead with obtaining the blood and urine cultures and fortunately, I was more successful with those procedures. Still, when I glanced at the clock as I was starting the baby's IV, I realized that I'd been at it for over an hour and I hadn't even ordered the antibiotics yet. Just then, the door to the treatment room flew open and the senior resident poked his head in.

"What are you doing in here? Aren't those antibiotics in yet?" he barked. He took another look at the baby, and I could tell he was as worried as I was. I tearfully explained that I'd had trouble with the LP and just hadn't been able to get any spinal fluid. He quickly and expertly had the nurse reposition the baby and before I knew it, he had the needle in and nice, clear spinal fluid coming out. I ran out to order the antibiotics. Thirty minutes later, they arrived from the pharmacy and the nurse gave them to the baby through the IV I'd started. Total time elapsed since he'd arrived on the unit: two hours. And in that time period, he'd become critically ill. His breathing became more labored and he needed to be put on a respirator. His blood pressure fell and his blood filled with lactic acid.

We worked on him for the rest of that long night, trying all sorts of medications and respirator changes, but he just didn't respond to anything we did. At 4:30 in the morning, his heart stopped and we just couldn't get him back. His parents held him and each other, sobbing and moaning behind the curtain of grief. Everyone suspected overwhelming sepsis, and I saw several staff members with tears in their eyes. And I just kept thinking, if only I'd been more competent and had gotten those antibiotics into him faster, maybe he'd have had a chance. The senior resident confirmed my terrible guilt.

"With sepsis, Chris," he admonished, "speed is of the essence. You've just got to get those antibiotics in quickly if you're going to have a chance to save 'em. I wish you'd paged me when you were having trouble with the LP."

At that moment, I decided that I should quit my residency and do something else with my life. Clearly I was not cut out to be a pediatrician. This was my very first admission as an intern, and my incompetence and poor judgment had led to a baby's death.

I spent the remainder of the night mindlessly completing all those tasks on my "to do" list that had been put off while I was busy with Owen (his parents told us his name only as they were leaving the unit after he'd died). But my heart was so heavy and I was so tired, I wasn't able to concentrate on anything. I kept thinking about Owen and his parents. As daylight arrived and the rest of the team started coming in for morning rounds, I just wanted to go home. But when there's been a terrible night in the NICU, everyone wants to know about it, and so I was pressed for all the gory details. It was so hard to talk about it, knowing how guilty I was and also knowing the decision I'd made about my future as a pediatrician. Somehow I got through rounds and began the daily work, which would keep me at the hospital until evening sign-out rounds at 5 P.M.

Earlier on that terrible night, I had called the baby's pediatrician, Dr. Roman, to let him know what was going on. He was as shocked as the rest of us were; there had been no problems with the pregnancy, the labor, or the delivery, and the baby had looked perfectly normal on his first exam in the nursery. But we all knew that sepsis can suddenly overwhelm a perfectly normal baby. After my phone call, he came in to see the baby and to help explain things to the terrified parents. And after the baby had died, he sat with the parents for quite some time, answering their questions and holding their hands. I was to learn later that he had brought up the sensitive issue of an autopsy at that time, and that the parents had agreed to have one done, hoping to find out more about what had happened to their little boy.

I was bone tired when I finally got home. All I wanted to do was to crawl into bed and forget that my first night on call in the NICU had ever happened. But sometimes such heavy fatigue prevented me from getting to sleep, and that night I just lay there in bed, turning things over and over in my mind for what seemed like hours. I thought about all my years of medical school and what a struggle some of the classes had been for me. Maybe that should have been a sign—that I just wasn't cut out for this demanding profession. On the other hand, I had been drawn to it because I realized that I could really help people—sometimes in their darkest hours. But when I finally fell asleep, it was with an overwhelming feeling of incompetence and inadequacy. I believed that baby Owen had died because I'd been too slow in getting the septic workup done and getting his antibiotics in.

I awoke the next morning emotionally exhausted. I had made my decision—I would quit my pediatric residency training and do something else with my life. Ironically, the idea that kept popping into my head was to become a pathologist, focusing on autopsies. There, I reasoned, I couldn't make any fatal errors. But I knew I couldn't simply quit on the spot; I needed to stay with the program until someone could be found to take my place. Even though I was "just an intern," I knew that the hospital machinery depended upon each and every one of us to keep things going—especially at night. And probably more important, I didn't want to "stiff" one of my colleagues, making that intern be on call every other night. That's what happened whenever one of us got sick or (gasp!) pregnant.

So I went to work as usual that next day, going through all the motions of rounds and "to do" lists as though nothing momentous had happened. In the afternoon, though, I went to see the chief resident in his office. Steve was one of those people who just exuded confidence and authority—and he also had a sense of humor. He could laugh at himself. I don't think I appreciated that quality as much then as I do now. I poured out my whole story, ending with my decision to quit the residency. As chief resident, Steve had heard most of the story already, since the senior residents reviewed all the previous night's admissions with him and the department chairman at intake rounds the next morning. But he listened to me as though it was the first time he'd heard about the case.

When I was finished, we both looked at each other. He said, "Chris, you did the best you could. You're just an intern. The senior resident should have stayed with you and helped you out; after all, it was your very first admission. I know you feel terrible—we've all felt this way at one time or another. But you'd be making an even bigger mistake if you threw your whole career away over this one terrible experience." Even though he said all the right things and in a very comforting way, only one thing was clear to me. He believed, like I did, that I was responsible—at least in part—for this baby's death. The truth was, I *was* slow in getting the procedures done. And we were all taught that with sepsis, time was of the essence. I told Steve that my mind was made up and that I wanted to leave the program as soon as a replacement could be found.

As I was on my way back to the NICU, my pager went off. It was Dr. Roman, Owen's pediatrician. He was looking for me because he had the baby's autopsy results and he knew I'd be interested. I met him on the NICU and he silently handed me the report. I read the brief history, including the results of the septic workup, which included the elevated white blood cell count that had only added to our suspicion of sepsis. It was painful to read the pathologist's summary of the events of that terrible night. And then I came to the final two lines of the report: "Postmortem examination on this child revealed hypoplastic left ventricle with atresia of the mitral and aortic valves and coarctation of the aorta. The final cause of death was hypoplastic left heart syndrome."

Owen had died because he was born with a then-fatal congenital heart defect. It wasn't sepsis. It wasn't my fault. Tears rolled silently down my face as Dr. Roman told me that Owen was typical of babies who have this type of heart defect. They look perfectly normal as long as a fetal blood vessel called the ductus arteriosus stays patent, allowing oxygenated blood to get to their bodies despite the abnormal development of the heart. But when the ductus arteriosus closes, as it normally does in the first day or two of life, the baby with the heart defect becomes critically ill because now there's no way for oxygenated blood to get to the body. The medical team often thinks of sepsis first, just as we all did, because the baby is essentially in shock. But it's cardiac shock, not septic shock.

Relief washed over me in a way I had never experienced before.

It wasn't my fault. I went back to Steve's office to tell him two things: I was staying in the residency program, and I was thinking of becoming a pediatric cardiologist.

CHAPTER 3

Jazmine

Toward the end of my first year of pediatric residency, I was assigned for one month to the "Mac House" rotation. MacDonald House was the Obstetrics-Gynecology department building and one floor was devoted to delivering babies—approximately 4,000 of them each year. This was one of the busiest rotations of the residency. The pediatric resident attended all cesarean-section deliveries and any full-term delivery in which a problem was anticipated (most of these involved meconium-stained amniotic fluid). We were also in charge of all the normal newborns in the nursery, particularly those who didn't have an assigned pediatrician, which was the case for most of the 20 to 30 babies in our public university hospital nursery. We did the initial newborn exams on those babies, followed their feeding progress, talked to their mothers about "well baby care" and "anticipatory guidance," and did their discharge exams.

The Mac House beeper was like a hot potato. We residents couldn't wait to pass it off to the next resident when our shift was over. The beeper went off constantly, summoning the resident to attend deliveries (these were always stat pages), discharge newborns (at all hours of the day or night), or see a baby that just didn't look right. You knew that if you were carrying the Mac House beeper, you'd be paged every 10 minutes or so, on average.

One of the good things about Mac House was that you could pick up newborns for your own panel of "continuity" patients. When we started our residency training, we'd each been assigned to an attending-led clinic team (mine was the Orange Team). Once a week, we were allowed to leave our inpatient rotation and see patients in our continuity clinics for an afternoon. We usually saw about six patients during each session. They were scheduled just as they would be in a regular pediatrician's office, although a pediatrician would generally see at least twice as many kids as we did. If you picked up a newborn for your clinic during your internship year, you then had a chance to follow that child for three years and really get to know the child and the family. By this time, toward the end of my first year, I had about 30 kids on my "panel" of patients. I'd inherited most from one of last year's graduating residents. Only a handful of them were "mine," and even fewer were infants. These latter I had picked up during my rotations in the Emergency Department, where I'd quickly discovered that parents who didn't have a pediatrician often used the emergency room whenever their child had an acute illness. We'd try to get these parents to come to our continuity clinics for follow-up of their child's illness, and some of them stayed with us after that for their "well child care." Now, however, was my big chance to pick up some newborns.

I was finishing up my delivery room note on a big, healthy baby girl who'd had some fetal distress but had turned out fine, when the beeper went off again—this time for the nursery.

"This is Chris Gleason returning a page," I said to Rosie, the unit clerk who answered the nursery phone.

"One of the babies has a temp," Rosie said, "and the nurses want you to check her out."

I sighed. If the "temp" indicated a fever, and was not just due to overheating the baby, then I'd have to start a septic workup and transfer the baby to the neonatal unit for antibiotics. At night the baby would be transferred over to the unit for the workup, but during the day, when there was an intern assigned to the nursery (me), our colleagues in the neonatal unit expected us to get most of the workup done before transferring the baby. This would really slow down my morning routine — I had at least a dozen babies who needed discharge newborn physicals so they could go home with their mothers.

When I arrived back at the nursery, the nurses led me to a roly-poly black baby sucking on her fingers in a bassinet. She didn't look very sick but when I looked at her bedside chart, I saw that her latest temperature — 39 degrees C — had been circled in red. It was an axillary temperature, taken with the thermometer held under her arm. If she had been overheated (usually by overzealous parents wrapping the baby in three or four layers of clothing and blankets), then a rectal temperature would be normal, or at least significantly lower than the axillary temperature.

"Have you done a rectal temp?" I asked the head nurse hopefully.

"Of course, Chris; you know we always check that first," she said somewhat smugly. "And it was the same as the axillary temp — 39 degrees C."

So, no matter how good the baby looked, she would need a full septic workup: blood, urine, and spinal fluid cultures. Before I got started, I'd need to talk to her mother, not only to let her know what was going on, but to ask for her permission to do a spinal tap (to get a sample of spinal fluid) and a suprapubic bladder tap (to get a clean, uncontaminated sample of urine). After I finished the procedures, I'd need to start an IV for her antibiotics. Then, I'd have to call the chief resident to let him know an admission was coming, write a transfer note, and finally, wheel the baby over to the neonatal unit myself. If everything went smoothly, I could get the whole job done in an hour. If not, who knew?

The baby's mother's name—Alma King—was written on a card taped to the bassinet, along with the baby's sex, birth weight, and length. I noticed a blank space by the notation "Pediatrician" and realized that this might be a golden opportunity for me to pick up a newborn patient for my continuity clinic roster.

I asked Rosie, the nursery unit clerk, where I could find Alma King's room, and she directed me to a large, four-patient room at the end of the hall. I had to call out Ms. King's name in order to be sure I talked to the right mother. A large, weary-looking woman answered softly, "That's me." And then she furrowed her brow and asked, "Is there anything wrong?"

I introduced myself as the doctor taking care of all the babies in the nursery and then told her that her two-day-old baby girl had developed a fever.

"But you'd never know there was anything wrong with her," I reassured her worried mom. "She's just lying there happily sucking on her fingers as if she didn't have a care in the world."

"Could I have just held her too long and gotten her all heated up?" Alma asked hopefully, just as I had asked the nurse about the rectal temp.

"Well, that's not very likely," I said, trying to explain the similarity between the baby's rectal and axillary temperatures. "And with newborn babies, you can never be too careful. They can't tell us if something hurts. So when they have a fever, we always assume it's an infection and begin treatment with antibiotics. If it turns out to be a false alarm, then we can just stop the antibiotics and send her home."

"So, how are you going to find out if she has an infection?" her mother asked me quietly, looking down at her bedclothes, which she was now wringing in her hands.

I then explained the procedures I would need to do in order to get clean samples of her baby's blood, urine, and spinal fluid. She winced visibly when I explained the suprapubic bladder tap I'd need to do in order to get the urine sample.

"Do you really have to do that one?" she asked. "I can understand the blood test and the spinal tap, but it just sounds awful to me — you sticking a needle right through her stomach into her bladder."

Inwardly, I had to agree with her. Suprapubic bladder aspiration was one of the most barbaric neonatal procedures we ever had to do. But, as I explained to Ms. King, it was necessary if we wanted to get a clean sample, uncontaminated by organisms that normally existed on the skin or around the baby's tiny urethra.

"If we just tried to 'catch' a clean sample in her diaper or got a sample by putting a catheter into her bladder through her urethra, it would be really hard to interpret if the culture came back positive," I told her. "We'd wonder if she had a real bladder infection, which would mean 10 days of IV antibiotics, or if we'd just gotten a contaminated specimen."

She said she wanted to know all the risks involved with the procedure before she'd agree to let me do it. I realized that I'd seriously underestimated this woman when I'd walked into the room. Normally, parents would simply accept what we told them and ask where they should sign. But this baby's mother wanted to know more. I pulled over a chair and spent the next 15 minutes trying to convince her that the procedure was safe (and that yes, I'd done it myself at least a dozen times without any mishaps). In the end, though, she refused to give me her consent. She told me she was willing to accept the consequences; that is, her baby might have to stay in the hospital for 10 days of IV antibiotics just because we couldn't be confident that a positive urine culture from a catheterized specimen was "real."

I was impressed with this woman, but I was also annoyed and

impatient. I'd spent a total of 30 precious minutes of my time talking to her and to some extent, it was all for naught. And now I was far behind on my "to do" list for the day. I gathered up the signed consent form for the lumbar puncture (LP) and the unsigned one for the suprapubic bladder tap and headed for the door. She called after me.

"Take good care of my baby, Dr. Gleason. Her name's Jazmine and she's all I've got in the world."

I promised her I'd do my best and assured her that I'd tell her any initial results, which I expected back by the end of the day. The culture results would take at least 48 hours and the baby would be in the neonatal unit when those results came back. By then, her mother would have been discharged and the staff in the neonatal unit would be the ones to discuss those results and the treatment plan with her. Most likely, I'd never see her again. So much for picking up newborns for my clinic panel.

It didn't take me long to get the blood work done and to do the spinal tap on little Jazmine and start her IV. I wrote a brief note and her initial antibiotic orders, and then called the chief resident and told him I needed to send a baby over to the neonatal unit.

"Another hot one?" he asked.

"Well, as a matter of fact, yes. Maybe we need to check the thermostat in the nursery. This baby's totally fine. I'd be surprised if anything grew."

"So we have blood, urine, and CSF to check, right?" he asked.

"Well, sort of," I said. And I told him what had happened with the suprapubic bladder tap.

"The mom knows what's at stake here, right?" he said. "I mean, if there's a positive cath culture, we're going to have to treat the kid even if it's likely to be a contaminant. And then we'll have to work up the baby's kidneys and urinary tract, too—before she goes home."

I explained that she knew all that and she didn't care. She just didn't want me to stick a needle into her baby's bladder, and that was that.

So I wrote the transfer orders and wheeled the baby over to the neonatal unit, giving a brief verbal report to the intern who was admitting her. Once that was done, I walked back to the nursery and plunged into my long list of discharge physicals and parent teaching sessions (which were very brief: bring the baby in if he/she is hot, yellow, or stops eating). At four o'clock, I crossed the last name off my list and sank into a chair in the resident charting area to finish up some paperwork.

My paperwork was interrupted by two delivery room calls, so I didn't finish work until 6:30. I was off that night and couldn't wait to get home, take a long, hot shower, and pour myself a glass of wine. On my way to the hospital parking lot I was considering having cheese and crackers for dinner so I wouldn't have to stop at the grocery store, when I suddenly remembered that I'd promised Jazmine's mother that I'd give her the initial test results. I told myself that the intern from the neonatal unit had probably already talked to her and a visit from me would be a waste of time, but I'd promised her. I knew I'd have to go back to the hospital, call for the results, and then go talk to Alma King.

I decided to go to the neonatal unit first, instead of the nursery. I was hoping that the intern had gotten all the results and written them in the baby's chart, which would save me the hassle of having to track them down. I lucked out. Everything was right there in the baby's chart when I located it at the nurses' station. The white blood cell count looked fine and so did the spinal fluid. But the urinalysis had a few white cells and some blood and protein in it—not as many as you'd expect to see with a bladder infection, but still a bit suspicious. I walked by Jazmine's room on my way over to the nursery and saw her mother standing by the baby's little crib, talking to Janet, the intern on call. As I walked over to the bedside, I was startled to see Alma point to me and explain to the intern that "there's Jazmine's doctor, Dr. Gleason. She took good care of my baby in the nursery."

I felt a little burst of pride. She actually considered me to be her baby's doctor. Then I realized that maybe it was because the little pink card taped to the crib, which had the baby's name, weight, and birth date on it, now had my name listed on the previously blank "Pediatrician" line. Oh well, I thought, it doesn't matter how she decided that I was Jazmine's doctor. I was just glad that she had because now I had a chance to add a new baby to my continuity clinic panel, beating out the admitting intern on the unit.

I listened for a few minutes as Janet finished her explanation of the urine test results and answered Alma's questions. Then I told both of them that I would check on the culture results tomorrow and we could discuss the plans for Jazmine. Of course, that would really be the job of the daytime intern, but I wanted to do what a real pediatrician would do. I left feeling that I'd made the right decision to return to the hospital, in more ways than one.

The next day I couldn't wait to check Jazmine's test results, and I was thrilled when I saw that all the cultures were negative (or "no growth") so far. But my elation was short-lived; Jazmine's intern in the neonatal unit called me the following day to say that her urine culture had turned positive. Everyone suspected that the cause was a contaminant, both because the culture had been a "cath" specimen and because real positive cultures usually turned positive within 24 hours. But we all knew that we'd have to assume that it was real and that Jazmine would need IV antibiotics for another eight days. I reminded her mother that we usually did a couple of tests when babies finished antibiotics for bladder infections—just to make sure that they didn't have a kidney or bladder defect, both of which make it more likely for them to get another bladder infection.

For the next week, I checked in on Jazmine and her mother every day, usually after I'd finished my work at Mac House. Alma had been discharged the day after Jazmine had been admitted to the neonatal unit and she'd essentially moved in to Jazmine's room, sleeping on a foldout chair by her baby's crib. Jazmine continued to thrive, nursing well and going through only two IVs during her entire antibiotic course. As the last day of her antibiotics drew near, the team in the neonatal unit asked my opinion about doing those tests we usually did before babies went home. It was the first time I'd ever been "consulted" on one of my patients, and I felt a real thrill. I'd read as much as I could about neonatal urinary tract infections and bladder or kidney defects and had reached the conclusion that since Jazmine's infection wasn't likely to be real, the yield of these tests would likely be very low and we could forgo them.

I sat down with Alma to discuss my conclusions with her. I'd gotten to know her quite a bit better during Jazmine's hospitalization. She'd gradually shared a few details of her life with me, including the fact that the baby's father was in jail and that she was on welfare, but working on her high school equivalency diploma so that she could get a job and give Jazmine a better life than she'd had. She listened carefully as I explained why we usually did a renal ultrasound and a voiding cystourethrogram in babies who'd had a urinary tract infection. And she listened even more carefully as I explained why I didn't think we needed to do these tests on Jazmine.

"I trust you to make the best decision for my baby," she said, looking me straight in the eye. "That's why I chose you to be her doctor."

Suddenly my clinical judgment, based upon the "evidence" I'd gleaned from the medical literature, seemed pretty arbitrary. Did I trust my own judgment as much as she did? And then I asked myself a question that I've continued to ask in similar moments of professional self-doubt over the years: What would I do if this was *my* baby? And I felt very comfortable with my decision. I told the team on the neonatal unit that I didn't think we needed to do those tests, and that I'd discussed the plan with the baby's mother and she'd agreed. Jazmine would be discharged without any prophylactic antibiotics and without our performing the follow-up kidney tests—primarily because we all thought that the positive urine culture she'd had was most likely a false positive result. I would see the baby two weeks after discharge in my continuity clinic.

And so Jazmine became the first newborn in my continuity clinic. By the time I was a third-year resident, I'd accumulated over two dozen newborns during my hospital rotations, but Jazmine was my first and, as it turned out, my most memorable. When I saw her at the two-week checkup I'd arranged, I couldn't believe how big she'd gotten—a pound heavier than her birth weight already. I told Alma what a great job she was doing and answered her questions about things such as diaper rash and nighttime crying jags.

Alma brought her faithfully to all the scheduled "well child checks" and I carefully administered all the scheduled baby shots and blood tests. She got sick only once—with an ear infection when she was a year old. I'd picked up the reddened eardrum on her routine 12-month checkup, and Alma was relieved that I'd found an explanation for Jazmine's increased fussiness and pulling on her right ear. The rest of her physical was fine, at least according to the brief notes I'd made in her clinic record—something I was to pore over later on.

Three months later, I saw Jazmine again for her scheduled 15-month checkup. This was usually a pretty short visit, and the main event was the first MMR vaccine (measles, mumps, and rubella). I had a very busy schedule in clinic that day and Jazmine was the last patient on my list. It was close to five o'clock—closing time at the clinic—when I walked into the exam room and sat down across from Alma, who was holding Jazmine in her lap. In answer to my standard 15-month checkup questions, she told me that Jazmine had taken her first steps just a month ago and could now walk across the room without holding onto anything. She could say several words, including "mama," "hi," and "NO," and she was a picky eater—except when it came to ice cream. I reviewed her growth, which was excellent, and then went over the usual 15-month "anticipatory guidance" things with Alma, such as making sure all harmful household substances were out of Jazmine's reach—including boiling pots of water on the stove. I briefly examined Jazmine while she was in Alma's lap—I found that toddlers did much better with that approach than with my trying to lay them down and hold them still on the examining table—but I couldn't get a very good abdominal exam. Jazmine wasn't about to hold still, plus she was pretty ticklish. I told Alma that I'd done the important things on the exam, and that Jazmine had passed with flying colors. I'd postpone a thorough abdominal exam until her 18-month visit, when she might be a bit more cooperative.

As I got the syringe and vial out to give Jazmine her MMR shot, Alma said, "I nearly forgot to tell you, Dr. Gleason; she has a sore spot on the front of her thigh. I don't remember her hurting herself there and there's no bruise, but if I press on the spot, she says 'ow' and pulls her leg away. You reminded me of it when you got out the shot stuff, because you usually give her the shot in her leg."

I held Jazmine's chubby little leg in my lap and pressed on the spot Alma had indicated. Jazmine jerked her leg away and started to cry. I was perplexed. There was no irregularity of the bone, no swelling or bruise over that spot, and no sign of an injury above or below it either. I asked Alma to bring Jazmine out into the hall and put her down so I could see her walk. My clinic preceptor, Dr. Mack, happened to walk by as Alma put Jazmine down and walked a few feet away. Jazmine immediately toddled over to Alma's open arms—no problems at all.

"What's up, Chris?" Dr. Mack asked, looking at his watch. It was closing time, and I had to get over to the Emergency Department to begin my overnight shift. I told him what Alma had told me—which I'd confirmed myself. I also told him that I hadn't found anything wrong, although I suddenly remembered that I hadn't really done a complete exam, thinking of her abdomen. He reached down and scooped up Jazmine in his arms, playing with her for a minute so she'd relax. Then, he too pressed on the spot that Alma pointed out to him, and Jazmine once again pulled her leg away and started to cry.

"She needs an X-ray," Dr. Mack said, "just to be on the safe side."

I felt my insides turn suddenly cold. Could this be a sign of something bad? And had I missed it?

I rushed to the charting room to get an X-ray requisition and hurriedly filled it out.

"X-ray right leg; point tenderness over right anterior femur. Rule out bone lesion."

Dr. Mack knew I had to get to the ED. He said he'd take Alma and Jazmine over to radiology for the X-ray and promised he'd phone me with the results.

"What about her shot?" Alma asked, and I saw that she now directed her question at Dr. Mack, who had explained the need for the leg X-ray while I was filling out the requisition. He had such a wonderful bedside manner, and he'd clearly assumed the care of my patient. He was my preceptor, and of course this was the way it should be, but I suddenly felt very junior and inexperienced. It seemed pretty apparent to me, and I think to Alma, too, that now that the situation had gotten serious, a "real" doctor was needed.

"If everything's fine on the X-ray," Dr. Mack explained, "then

I'll give her the shot before you go home." Alma didn't ask what would happen if everything was not fine on the X-ray.

I said good-bye to Alma and Jazmine; Alma just waved distractedly at me and gazed anxiously at Jazmine's leg. I hurried over to the ED and plunged quickly into the stack of waiting patients—mostly kids with minor injuries and illnesses. I cleaned out lots of earwax on my ED shifts so that I could get a better look at the kids' eardrums. About two hours later I got a page, and when I called the number displayed on my beeper, Dr. Mack answered the phone. I braced for the worst, and I got it.

"She has a lytic bone lesion, Chris."

I felt as though the breath had just been sucked out of me.

"Where do you think the primary is?" I asked, referring to the metastatic tumor she must have. I tried not to let my emotions spill over into my voice, but tears were welling up in my eyes and I swallowed hard. Dr. Mack said that neuroblastoma was the most likely diagnosis; when it spread, it often went to the bone. Neuroblastoma was a tumor of the adrenal glands, which sat right above each kidney. I suddenly flashed back 15 months, to Jazmine's very first hospitalization. Could this cancer have been there when she was born? And, I thought irrationally, could we have seen it if we'd done that renal ultrasound—the test I'd recommended *not* doing because I thought it was so unlikely that she'd really had a bladder infection? It was an irrational thought, because I knew that although neuroblastoma could be diagnosed in newborns, it was usually considered because the baby had characteristic skin lesions—which Jazmine never had—and it's usually benign or at least eminently treatable. Unlike neuroblastoma in a toddler that had already spread to the bone, which was usually fatal.

Jazmine would be admitted that night to the toddler unit so that all the necessary tests could be done and treatment could be started—usually beginning with surgery and staging of the tumor.

As Dr. Mack went on, it was so clear to me that he was in charge, which was as it should be—he was my clinic preceptor and ultimately responsible for all my clinic patients. I told him that I would stop by Jazmine's room in the morning, after my ED shift was over. Dr. Mack said he was sure that Alma would appreciate that.

I did stop by Jazmine's room the next morning, carrying an extra Styrofoam cup of coffee in case Alma hadn't had a chance to get down to the cafeteria. Jazmine wasn't there. She was already in the operating room, having a thorough physical exam (no one else had been able to palpate her abdomen either) and various painful tests done—all under anesthesia.

Alma sat in the chair by Jazmine's crib, looking exhausted and dazed. She accepted the cup of coffee but didn't take a sip. She just held the warm cup in her hands and breathed in the steam.

"Do you think it was there when she was born?" she whispered, with despair in her voice. So she'd been thinking about that, too.

I confessed that I'd had the same thought, but I told her what I knew to be true: that neuroblastoma in the newborn just doesn't present that way.

"That's what Dr. Mack told me," she said, "but I just wanted to ask you because you were there back then. You were her very first doctor."

The only word I really heard was *were*. We both knew I wasn't going to be her doctor anymore, and I felt a deep sense of loss.

"She was my very first newborn continuity patient," I told Alma then.

"I knew that," Alma said. "The nurses in the nursery explained how we could pick one of you training doctors to be our baby's doctor if we wanted. I picked you because you had such a nice face, and you spent so much time with me, explaining about Jazmine's fever and everything. And I wish you could still be her doctor—her cancer doctor."

I assured her that I would still be her doctor—for her "well child care" once she became well again. And of course I told her that I would visit whenever Jazmine was in the hospital. In those days, most pediatric cancer care took place in the hospital, not in the outpatient setting, as it does today. I knew I would have lots of chances to visit Jazmine and her mother.

Alma put down her coffee cup and reached out to grasp both of my hands in hers.

"Pray for my baby, Dr. Gleason," she pleaded. "Pray for her hard."

Jazmine died six months later in the Pediatric ICU, held tightly in her mother's arms.

CHAPTER 4

Linda

IN JULY 1980, I became a second-year resident and was assigned to my first rotation in the Pediatric Intensive Care Unit (PICU). Interns weren't considered experienced enough for this grueling rotation, which involved being "on call" every other night for a month and caring for complex cases of critically ill children ranging in age from one month to 18 years. Although there were fewer patients than in the NICU (an average of 10 compared to 30), there were more diagnoses to consider, and the different developmental stages of the children presented unique challenges to their caretakers. During that rotation, I took care of children with severe asthma, meningitis, head injuries (sometimes intentional), severe pneumonia, diabetic ketoacidosis, epiglottitis, complex congenital heart disease, and a little-understood condition called Reye's syndrome. During my first week, six patients died, and I began to realize that death was a more likely outcome in the PICU than in the NICU. And I also realized that for me, there was an important difference between caring for critically ill neonates who'd been in the hospital from birth and older infants or children who'd been admitted to the hospital from home. Every detail of the NICU baby's life was known to us, whereas the older children in the PICU had a whole life outside the hospital before we ever met them.

Linda was a 14-year-old with chronic asthma. Her condition had been diagnosed when she was two, and she'd had numerous admissions to the hospital since then for bad asthma attacks. We measured severity of asthma by how many times a child needed to be in the PICU (to be on a respirator) and by that measure, Linda was one of the worst. Her PICU admissions were "TNTC"—too numerous to count. In addition to daily pills, Linda used an inhaler to control her asthma symptoms at home and at school. Each puff of the inhaler delivered a powerful burst of a bronchodilator medication that could relieve the spasms of her breathing passages—the hallmark of asthma. There were powerful side effects, too, such as increased heart rate and heart strain. Inhaler use was limited by these side effects—no more than a certain number of puffs were allowed each day. When she was younger, her parents were in charge of the inhaler, making sure Linda used it only when she needed it. But now that Linda was a teenager, she was in charge. And like most teenagers, she didn't always use it responsibly.

The day I was to meet Linda in the PICU had started uneventfully for her. She'd woken up feeling fine—got dressed, ate a typical teenage breakfast (PopTart, orange juice), and took her daily medications. She had a minor argument with her father, went to school, and by all accounts, had a good day—including an invitation to the homecoming dance from a junior boy, definitely a big deal for a freshman. She spent a couple of hours with friends after school, painting each other's toenails. Sometime during that afternoon, though, she began wheezing and feeling "tight" in her chest. Perhaps it was the nail polish, or perhaps anxiety about the upcoming dance.

She started using her inhaler—her friends later said they saw her use it several times. No one was sure how many. When she got home, her mother noticed that she looked a bit pale and tired, but Linda said nothing about her wheezing earlier that afternoon, and nothing about her use of the inhaler. She said she had a lot of homework and went up to her room to get started on it before dinner. An hour later, her mother called her for dinner and when Linda didn't respond, she went upstairs and knocked on her door. When there was no answer, she walked in. As soon as she saw Linda, struggling to breathe and using her inhaler, she knew she was in trouble with another asthma attack. She'd had so many similar attacks in the past; neither she nor her mother felt that this one was any different. But they both knew she'd need to go to the hospital. Linda's father had just arrived home from work, and they decided that he would take her while Linda's mother finished serving dinner to her younger brother and sister. Linda packed up a few things to bring along with her in case she would be admitted to the hospital—her pink stuffed rabbit, her lucky charm bracelet, and her homework. And she kept using the inhaler, even though by now her heart was racing.

Linda walked into the ER with her father. Later, when she was in the PICU, that image too often came to mind.

The triage nurse did a quick exam, noting her pale color, rapid heart rate, and labored breathing. She put her in an exam room right away, placed an oxygen mask on her, and hooked her up to an electrocardiograph monitor. At least, everyone said later, she didn't sit for hours in the waiting room. Linda sat quietly, hunched over and trying to breathe, and reached for her inhaler. Her father questioned her then about how many times she'd used it in the last hour, but she just shrugged her shoulders. By this time, her chest was so tight, she couldn't speak. When the doctor—John, one of my fellow residents—came in, she quickly put the inhaler into her jacket pocket. He began asking her some questions and she just nodded her head yes or no. So he started to examine her and, he later remembered, was alarmed by her shallow, labored breathing, her rapid pulse rate, and the bluish tinge on her lips despite the oxygen mask.

John decided that she needed an arterial blood gas test done to determine how low her oxygen level was (there were no skin oxygen sensors in those days) and how high her carbon dioxide level was. He knew both were indicators of just how severe an attack was, and would be used to decide whether a child would go right to the PICU or be admitted to one of the regular wards. Linda had had this test done many times and knew that it involved a somewhat painful needle puncture on her wrist, over her radial artery. If the needle went right into the artery, it wasn't too bad, but if it took several tries, it could hurt like hell.

As John was on his third attempt, Linda suddenly collapsed and nearly fell off the exam table. At first John thought she'd fainted, but then he realized she wasn't breathing. And the EKG monitor began to alarm; her rapid heart rate had slowed to a near standstill. She'd "arrested" or "Coded," as we called it. John shouted for help and a few minutes later, a "Code Blue" was called over the hospital loudspeaker, summoning the arrest team from around the hospital.

I heard the Code called while I was eating a sandwich in the PICU staff lounge. I sighed, because I knew it meant I'd be getting an admission—if the patient could be successfully resuscitated, that is. Sure enough, about 30 minutes later, I answered a page from the senior admitting resident. He, along with the PICU fellow, was on the arrest team and had led the efforts to resuscitate Linda. He gave me a very brief synopsis of what had happened and told me to start getting things ready to "put lines in." Sometimes it seemed as though that's all we ever did when kids were admitted to the PICU—insert catheters into arteries and central veins. Although these "lines" allowed blood tests to be obtained more easily and monitored heart and respiratory function more closely, they often took a lot of time to put in, and during that time, no one seemed to be thinking about what was wrong with the patient. This proved to be the case with Linda. When she arrived in the PICU, she was immediately hooked up to one of the unit's respirators and the single IV line she had was connected to a couple of standard "drips"—dextrose and dopamine. For the next two hours, we put in the other lines. Each time we got one in, I wrote new drip orders—for additional medications and for solutions needed to keep the lines open and functioning well, for as long as we needed them. Linda was completely motionless at first, but then she began twitching—first around her mouth and eyelids and then, her hands and feet. I thought she was reacting to the numerous needle punctures. But the PICU fellow and senior resident said no, she was probably having seizures, which were relatively common after a cardiac arrest. We all hoped that her twitching wasn't clonus. Clonus was a bad sign after an arrest. It meant that neurons were simply firing off electrical impulses wildly, without any input signal. I wrote new orders for large doses of several anti-seizure medications and for muscle relaxants, the latter just so we would have a better chance of getting our lines in.

At some point, I was sent down to Linda's feet to try to put in another central venous line using the large "intern's vein" just above the inner ankle bone. And it was then that I first took in her toenails. They'd been freshly painted that afternoon and there they were, glowing red, staring me in the face. To me, those toenails were a neon sign of the real life Linda had been living just hours before everything became unreal.

I got the long intravenous line in on my first attempt and I felt that wonderful glow of success that I always got—and still do—when I performed a procedure well. But this glow felt very different from the feeling I got placing an umbilical vessel catheter in a newborn preemie. Those polished toenails meant that Linda had belonged to many other people before she belonged to us in the PICU. Even though newborns in our NICU most often came with loving, terrified parents, grandparents, aunts, uncles, and godparents, they hadn't really *lived* a life outside the NICU. Their lives outside the uterus began with us. Now I was faced with a stark reality—here was a teenage girl, just like me a decade earlier, who was now being "worked on" by this team of people. And some of us were beginning to realize that things might not turn out so well. Linda was showing signs of clonus.

For the next few days, we took care of all of Linda's body systems. The asthma attack that had caused all the problems in the first place quickly responded to all the usual therapies and she didn't develop pneumonia to complicate matters. Her blood pressure was stable and her heart showed no signs of permanent damage, although she had clearly strained this important muscle with her excessive inhaler use. Her bowels began to function, and we placed a feeding tube into her stomach through which we put a liquid formula that contained "all the major food groups," as we explained to her parents. She got her period. Her toenails continued to grow and her nail polish began to recede.

But Linda did not wake up. She didn't open her eyes or squeeze her mother's hand in response to her whispered entreaties. We played her favorite tapes and she never responded. The neurologists were consulted and various tests were done to determine her level of brain functioning. The answer was terrible—for us and for her parents. She had no meaningful brain function. Her pupils were "fixed and dilated." She was brain dead. The period of time during which her heart had nearly stopped had deprived her brain of oxygen and energy long enough to basically kill it. I'd been in the PICU long enough to see at least a dozen children die and each time, I shared a small sliver of the family's huge pain. I just couldn't imagine how they coped, and yet they all did, each in their own way. Somehow, I felt more of the pain of Linda's death. I watched silently as her friends came to say good-bye. They, too, could not understand how their bubbly, wise-cracking friend could suddenly wind up like this, from just an asthma attack. Even an accident was easier to accept somehow. Didn't we all say at one time or another, "you never know, you could be hit by a truck"?

After agonizing over the decision, her parents agreed to take Linda off life support and to donate her organs for transplant, hoping that someone else could live because of the tragedy that had happened to her. On the day this was being planned, her best friend, Lisa, came by for a last visit. A full week had gone by since that terrible night. Lisa stood silently by the foot of the bed for a while, gazing at her friend's face, the quiet rise and fall of her chest as the respirator breathed for her, and finally, at her feet.

I watched from across the room as Lisa took a bottle of nail polish from her purse and carefully touched up the toenail polish on her best friend's feet. I just couldn't help myself. Right there in the middle of the PICU, tears began to roll down my cheeks and I began blubbering like a baby. I had to leave the room to regain my composure. It just wouldn't do to have staff and family members see "the doctor" bawling her eyes out. But I never forgot that scene. And it was really at that moment that I knew I could never become a pediatric intensivist. I loved intensive care, but I needed to take care of new babies—not older children who came to me already having lived a life outside the hospital that I couldn't save. I would become a neonatologist.

CHAPTER 5

Patrick

"HE'S JUST WAY too small to survive, Chris," explained Carlos, the senior neonatal fellow who had rushed over to attend this precipitous delivery with me. We both stared at the tiny baby whom I'd just deposited onto the warmed resuscitation table, fresh from the womb. I was a second-year pediatric resident and I had just started another in a series of one-month rotations on the preemie unit, known as "7P." I'd attended several dozen deliveries of premature babies since I'd started my internship and I had to agree that this was by far the smallest baby I'd ever seen. And yet...there was something about this tiny baby that was different from the others. For one thing, he had his eyes wide open. The eyes of extremely premature babies are usually fused shut, like a kitten's. And another thing—this baby was flailing his little arms and legs around and breathing on his own, without any help from us. In my limited experience with very premature babies, that just didn't happen.

We'd been stat paged to this delivery without knowing many details about the pregnancy beforehand. All we knew was that the baby's mother was young and had been rushed to the emergency room with severe abdominal pain and a blinding headache. Her blood pressure was sky high and while the ER staff rushed to treat her hypertensive crisis before she had a stroke, an astute resident had thought to quickly do an abdominal ultrasound and discovered that she was pregnant—something she had vigorously denied. When she began having seizures, she was quickly transferred to Labor and Delivery for an emergency cesarean section. The diagnosis was presumed to be toxemia and if the baby wasn't delivered quickly, no matter how premature, she could die.

Suddenly, I thought I heard some squeaky, mewing noises coming from the baby's mouth. Was this tiny human actually crying? Carlos and I looked at each other. He had heard it, too. And then incredibly, a tiny stream arced upward from the baby's miniature penis. This was a real, live baby boy. What should we do? Should we begin the standard resuscitation procedures? Intubate him? Put him on a ventilator?

"Why don't we weigh him?" Carlos suggested. This would not only give us more time to make a decision about what to do next, it would also answer the first question the attending neonatologist would likely ask us if we admitted the baby to the preemie unit. So, I put a blanket down on that cold infant scale and zeroed it, which would subtract the weight of the blanket from the readout of the baby's weight. Then I gingerly picked up the baby—he nearly fit in the palm of my hand—and laid him gently on the scale. Neither of us could believe it. The dial read 450 grams, including the plastic clamp around his umbilical cord. It couldn't be true, I thought. He weighed just under one pound. An article had recently appeared in one of the pediatric medical journals questioning whether we were doing anyone any favors by resuscitating premature babies weighing less than 800 grams. This baby weighed barely half that.

"Dr. French will have a fit if we bring this baby over to the unit," Carlos said. "We don't even have an endotracheal tube small enough for his trachea, if he needed to go on a ventilator. And he'll probably have a major head bleed and wind up devastated—if he lives, that is."

That was a big if, but still, there he was, looking at us, squeaking and breathing on his own. What choice did we really have? And what would we do with him if we didn't take him with us back over to 7P? His mother was still under general anesthesia and as far as we knew, no one had come with her to the hospital. There would be no one to hold him if we decided to let him go.

"What harm would there be in just bringing him over and putting him in an incubator? We could try putting in umbilical catheters," I added hopefully. These catheters, if we were successful in getting them in, would allow us to monitor the baby and to obtain blood tests without "sticking" him. They could also be used to give him IV medications and fluids—all of which would be essential, because it would be a long, long time before he could take enough milk to nourish his tiny body.

"I'll take full responsibility for bringing him over," I offered, suspecting that Carlos would be raked over the coals for having "resuscitated" such a tiny baby with such a terrible prognosis—even though we hadn't yet done anything to him or for him. "If he goes down the tubes, we'll just let him go. And if he hangs in there…" I couldn't finish the sentence because I really didn't know what we'd do—what *I'd* do—if this baby made it. None of the equipment we had in the Neonatal ICU in those days was designed for babies this small.

"Well, okay then, he's all yours," said Carlos, and I thought I detected a note of relief in his voice. Apparently he also couldn't imagine just leaving the baby all alone in a little bassinet off in a corner of the delivery room to die.

So that's how Patrick, as I later decided to call him, became "my baby" during my rotation on 7P that month. I did have some explaining to do when the double doors to the unit swung open and I wheeled in this incredibly small baby. But I could tell that even Dr. French could see, as he peered through the incubator's Plexiglas walls, that this baby was different. He was so active, so alive, and he clearly had no lung disease. He did become prone to frequent attacks of apnea in which he simply forgot to breathe, a common problem of prematurity. In addition to starting him on caffeine (which stimulates the baby's brain breathing center), we used a "bumper bed." We don't use these beds anymore, but in those days, babies prone to apnea could be placed on a special mattress that automatically inflated and deflated so that the baby would be "shaken up" every minute or so and therefore reminded to breathe. Those bumper beds took the place of the nurses who would flick the babies' heels or gently shake the babies whenever the apnea alarm sounded. Every now and then during morning rounds, someone would feel the urge to push the button that manually inflated the mattress, and while we discussed various medical issues, the baby would go up and down in his incubator, often with a startled look in his eyes.

I did manage to get catheters into the incredibly tiny blood vessels in his umbilical cord—one in the vein that we used to give him fluids and nutrition, and one in the artery that we used to monitor his blood pressure and heart rate and to draw any needed blood tests. It was a good thing, too, because we all agreed that there was no way anyone could have gotten an IV into one of his tiny, thready veins—not even me, who by then had a reputation as the resident who could "start an IV in a tree." If I hadn't gotten those catheters in, we would have had no choice but to feed him, and his poor little intestines probably couldn't have handled it. We left those catheters in for three weeks, even though he didn't need them after he was able to tolerate "full" milk feedings at two weeks of age. No one wanted to take a chance that we'd need to draw blood or administer an IV medication like an antibiotic. We all held our breath the day those catheters came out, and we sighed with relief for many subsequent days when he didn't get sick or throw up his feedings.

After he'd survived the first week with no catastrophes, everyone agreed that he was most likely a runt, or "IUGR" as we termed babies who had been intrauterine growth restricted—usually due to the constricting effects of high maternal blood pressure on the placenta's blood vessels, which then limits the amount of oxygen and nutrients that can be delivered to the developing fetus. His birth weight of 450 grams was the average weight for a 22-week gestation fetus, an age considered to be nonviable back in 1980 and even by most neonatologists today. But Patrick acted like a much more mature baby—perhaps even as far along as 32 weeks—who was just small for his age—very, *very* small.

When Patrick was three days old, I decided I needed to spend some time with his mother, letting her know the essentials of what was going on with her tiny son. I'd briefly visited her postpartum room several hours after the delivery, when she'd awoken from the general anesthetic but was still sick and groggy, in part due to the drugs she'd been given to control her blood pressure and to treat the seizures she'd had. When I'd briefly introduced myself as her baby's doctor, she'd just closed her eyes and turned her head away. This time, when I walked into her room, she was sitting up in bed, sipping something from a Styrofoam cup and watching a soap opera on television. I reintroduced myself as her baby's doctor and asked her if this was a good time to talk. She shrugged her shoulders, which I took as a "yes," but she continued staring at the TV while I pulled up a chair next to her bed.

I asked her to please turn off the TV while we talked, and she obliged with a deep sigh. I knew from having read her now more complete medical chart, and from talking to the social worker, that she was 20 years old, single, and a junior at a local college. She had continued to deny that she'd even suspected she was pregnant, and considering how small the baby was and how large she was—someone had described her as "zoftig"—that particular detail wasn't too surprising. I had also read that she wasn't sure who the father of her baby was—she'd had a couple of boyfriends in the past six months. And finally, that her parents, an affluent divorced couple who lived in separate states, were as shocked as she was to discover her pregnancy but were relieved that their daughter was going to be all right. No one had visited the baby yet.

When I asked her what she'd heard so far about her baby, she responded by saying, "Look, I've decided to give him up for adoption. There's no way I could take care of a baby right now or raise a child. I'm signing the papers as soon as they're ready. I don't want to get too attached, so I don't really want to know anything about him and I don't want to see him either.

"Unless he's going to die," she suddenly added.

"But at the moment," I explained, "you are his only legal guardian, and until an adoptive family has been chosen or the state takes temporary custody, you're the only person who could consent to any procedures he might need, like surgery." I wasn't entirely sure of this, and I made a mental note to ask the social worker for more details, but I wanted to be able to tell her something about this amazing little baby I was caring for in the unit, and this seemed to be the only way for me to pique her interest.

It worked. After a brief pause, she told me that she knew she'd had a boy, that he was incredibly small, weighing less than a pound, and that he was still alive. "How is that possible?" she asked me. "And what will happen to him? Will he ever be normal?"

I certainly didn't have all the answers to her questions, especially not as a second-year resident, but I did try to explain the concept of IUGR—relating it to her hypertension—and I briefly outlined some of the typical preemie things that could be expected to happen during the next several weeks, or months, that he would likely be in the hospital; that is, if he pulled through and didn't get a serious infection, or necrotizing enterocolitis, a terrible condition in which a preemie's intestines can suddenly become gangrenous.

When I'd finished, there was a long silence, which was finally broken when she thanked me and said she'd do whatever we needed her to do legally regarding the baby. She reiterated her decision about adoption and said her mother supported her in this, and had told her it would be best for her not to see the baby. I told her I understood and would of course respect her decision.

As I got up and pushed my chair back from her bed, I just couldn't help myself. I had to add, "You know, no one in this hospital has ever seen a baby this small survive for this long, and not even need to be on a ventilator. Your son is a pretty miraculous little guy. We're all rooting for him."

She nodded, and I thought I glimpsed a brief, proud smile. Then she flipped the TV back on and returned to her soap opera. I never saw her again, but I did hear from one of the nurses that she had stopped by the unit the night before her discharge from the hospital and spent a few minutes staring at her son, lying in his incubator. She said she was too scared to touch him, but at least she saw him. I've often wondered how she's remembered that moment. Did she cherish it? Did she regret it? Did she wish she'd spent more time with him?

The baby continued to thrive, and we all marveled at his progress. Most of the other residents in my training program had heard about him at morning report, during coffee breaks after morning rounds, and late at night when we were on call. In a way, this baby, this "micropreemie" as we began to refer to him, offered a bit of positive counterbalance to the generally negative feelings that most of my fellow residents had about preemies. In those days, most of the littlest ones died, sometimes after what seemed to us to be painful, futile efforts to save them. And the ones who lived often seemed to have suffered devastating injuries—especially to their brains. We all held our breath as Patrick's head ultrasound was being done, and there was a collective sigh of relief as we saw no brain bleeding or other signs of serious brain injury such as a stroke. He didn't get NEC or sepsis or chronic lung disease, either. He just grew, doubling his birth weight in only four weeks. Dr. French asked the team during attending rounds one day to try to imagine what it would feel like, what it would *look* like, to double our weight—in just one month.

I felt as though he was partially mine. After all, I was the one who had brought him over from the delivery room. I took pride in his little accomplishments: when he was weaned off the bumper bed and the caffeine and remembered to breathe; when he started taking his feedings from a bottle; when he "passed" his first eye exam. Many of the unit staff and some of the other residents started to feel the same way I did. When everyone realized that he would be going up for adoption, choosing a temporary name for him became a free-for-all. It was a wonderful distraction from the hard work that absorbed us. Some people picked boy names popular at the time, such as Andrew, Brian, or Jason. Others thought his name should be unique, like him, and favored names like Ulysses, Lincoln, and Adonis. And then there were the nicknames. "Peanut" was the most popular, but there was also "Shoe Box" (from that old story of Winston Churchill being a preemie cared for in a shoe box placed on the stove) and of course "Lucky," like the last surviving puppy in *101 Dalmatians*.

But I chose Patrick, and somehow it seemed to stick. I had read about Patrick Bouvier Kennedy, the barely premature (at 36 weeks' gestation) infant son of John and Jackie Kennedy, who had died of premature lung disease at three days of age in the basement of Boston Children's Hospital in 1963. It seemed like a perfect tribute to name this tiny baby, who seemingly was surviving against all odds, for the Kennedys' lost son.

At the end of the month, I left 7P to start a new rotation on the pediatric surgery service. One late night when I was on call, I stopped by to see one of the surgical patients in the unit and there he was, outside of his incubator, being held by one of the nurses as he hungrily fed from a bottle. He was six weeks old and now weighed two and a half pounds. His face looked like a little old man's, and he was all skin and bones. But he had that same alert, interested look in his eyes that I'd seen in the delivery room. I asked the nurse if I could hold him, and she handed him to me while someone snapped a Polaroid. I still have that picture and when I look at it, I'm struck again by how miraculous his early life was, and also by how much I've changed. And I wonder what he's doing now.

Everyone said they wanted to adopt him. Most weren't serious. Gradually, though, we realized that Jessica, one of his "primary" nurses, *was* serious. She and her husband had tried for several years to get pregnant and had finally been successful, using powerful fertility drugs. But their triplet girls had been born prematurely and tragically, one by one, they had all died—and in this very unit. When I first brought Patrick over from the delivery room, it was difficult for the charge nurse to find a nurse to assign him to. Most of the nurses, and indeed most of the physician staff, thought he was way too small and would probably just get the "dwindles" and die—especially when it was made very clear that no one, not even me, was going to put an endotracheal tube in him to put him on a ventilator. But Jessica was working the day he was born, and after she'd peered briefly into the incubator, she said she'd do it. Later, she told me that the baby seemed to look right at her and she felt an instant bond.

When Jessica came back to work in the unit the day after Patrick was born, and saw that he was still alive, she asked if she could be assigned to care for him. From then on, whenever she wasn't needed for a "one-to-one" critically ill baby, she asked to have

Patrick on her nursing assignment list. She got to know him the way mothers got to know their preemies — tentatively at first, but gradually trusting their own instincts. We, and the nursing staff, learned to rely on parents' intuition regarding their babies. We paid attention when a mother said things like "he's just not right today" or "something's bothering her." Jessica started to act that way about Patrick, and she started referring to him as "my baby." She started phoning in on the days she wasn't working, to see how he was doing. Once she left a note for me, taped to his incubator, asking me to order something for his diaper rash, which she was sure was yeast (she was right). She found some nonfrilly, blue baby-doll clothes and after washing them several times so they'd be soft and safe, she'd dress him up after a bath and take some pictures. She held him the way seasoned mothers, over their initial fright, would hold their babies to comfort them. So none of us was surprised when she and her husband began talking in earnest to the social worker on his case about adopting him.

Nearly three months after he was plucked from his mother's womb to save her life, Patrick was ready to go home. He weighed three and a half pounds, less than most preemies do at the time of discharge, but he remembered to breathe; he could take all of his feedings from a bottle; and his penis had grown enough that he could be safely circumcised. His mother had chosen Jessica and her husband to be his adoptive parents and although the legal proceedings weren't finalized yet, they could take him home and begin life as a family. As the day grew closer, I realized that I would be on vacation when Patrick went home, so I went up to 7P to say goodbye. Jessica was working that day and she had put another cute little outfit on him. He had graduated to a bassinet, just like the ones that full-term babies go into after they're born, and he looked so tiny in it. I picked him up and carried him over to a nearby rocking chair and sat down with him. As I rocked him slowly back and forth, our eyes met and he stared at me intently. It was as though there was a brief moment of recognition, making me think about those stories of "imprinting" that are popular in magazines like *Scientific American*. These were the same eyes that had looked directly at me just a couple of months ago, eyes that made me hope that this baby was a "keeper" despite his unbelievably small size.

Jessica and her husband decided to keep the name Patrick, much to my delight. Although I saw lots of pictures of him on the 7P bulletin board after he left the hospital, I saw him only once before I left Cleveland to start my fellowship. He had an appointment with one of the pediatric ophthalmologists at the hospital, who was treating his "lazy eye." Jessica brought him up to 7P for a brief visit and I happened to be the senior resident on the team. He was almost 18 months old and was obviously still small for his age. I guessed that he weighed maybe 15 pounds with all his clothes on, and he was very short, just coming up to his mother's knees. But he seemed right on track developmentally. With a shock of thick black hair, he pulled at his mother's hand, jumped up and down, and tried to touch everything within reach or within eyeshot. "Wanna see it!" he shouted. "Wanna touch it." Your basic normal toddler.

I thought back to that day in the delivery room when Carlos and I debated whether we should bring him over to the unit or just wrap him up and let him go. It was such a life-and-death decision, and yet it seemed so arbitrary at the time. We were so afraid that he would die after painful, futile efforts to keep him alive — or worse, survive, only to wind up severely disabled and with no one who wanted to care for him. If we'd been able to see into a crystal ball and to know that he would turn out so amazingly well, our decision would have been so much easier.

Suddenly, Patrick escaped from his mother's tight grasp and made a beeline for a procedure tray with loads of shiny bright instruments on it. I went after him and scooped him up before he knocked the whole thing over. As I held him firmly against my hip, he reached out with his little hands and tried to push himself away from me, shouting "NO!" and "Wanna play with it!" I looked at him and as those still remarkably familiar eyes glared back at me, I realized something that has helped me ever since in making similar difficult decisions. In the end, it was really Patrick who had decided his own fate in the delivery room. He was simply doing too well to leave there. And even in the unit, he ultimately determined his course and we just cared for him as he moved along from milestone to milestone, just as his parents were caring for him now. If he'd gotten septic or had developed that severe intestinal disease NEC, he would have died. But he didn't. And I hope he is having a wonderful life.

CHAPTER 6

Hannah

MORNING ROUNDS were over and our team of interns, residents, and med students were all sitting at "our" table in the cafeteria, having coffee and doughnuts. I loved those times, because it felt so normal—not like the chaos and uncertainty of the wards and the patients we were dealing with. We often told stories from our nights on call, usually with a heavy dose of gallows humor thrown in. Physicians, nurses, and hospital staff all used the same cafeteria as patients' families, so we had to be careful not to use names or to speak too loudly.

Larry, the senior resident, was carrying on about an encounter he'd had with one of the nurses. She'd called him a bimbo after he'd accidentally pulled out an IV he'd finally gotten in—after 10 attempts. We were discussing her choice of insulting words when we heard "Code Blue—7 West" paged three times on the hospital PA system. We all froze for a second and then leapt up and ran for the stairs (you really couldn't wait for the elevator to come). Our unit was 7 West—the infant intensive care floor. Our patients ranged in age from newborns to one-year-olds, which made it different from the NICU or preemie unit, as we called it. The infants on 7 West had a variety of problems, including birth defects, serious infections, and nutritional or respiratory problems. Some babies had been there since birth with chronic diseases resulting from prematurity. Hannah was one of those babies. She'd been born at 30 weeks' gestation and unfortunately had developed necrotizing enterocolitis when she was only two weeks old. Surgery saved her life, but left her with "short gut" syndrome. She had barely enough intestines left to survive and was still hooked on intravenous nutrition, now at one year of age. But mentally, her development was right on target. She could now pull herself to a stand and had mastered several words—most notably "IV," which generally made her cry.

When we arrived on the ward, breathless from our stair climb, we headed straight for the intensive care room, where we expected to find our Code patient. This room had the most critically ill babies. Most of them were on ventilators. But the chaos all seemed to be coming from the next room down the hall—Hannah's room. Oh no, I thought. Something's happened to Hannah. Maybe she got an air bubble in her central line. Maybe she's gotten septic. You always think about the worst-case scenarios when you're called stat to some sort of crisis or Code. But none of us was prepared for what was going on in that room.

We all rushed in and there, lying inert on the floor, with two nurses doing CPR, was a well-dressed elderly woman. Someone's grandmother? I thought. A heart attack? We were momentarily stunned, and then we sprang into our standard Code roles. This is what we'd been trained to do automatically, without really thinking much about what we were doing. It reminded me of the military. Larry, as the most senior resident, "ran" the Code. He had the nurses pause their chest compressions so that he could check the woman's carotid artery for a pulse. He couldn't detect one. He then started barking out orders. "Keep going with that mouth-to-mouth breathing. We don't have an adult-size mask or an Ambu bag to ventilate her. And we certainly can't intubate her with our infant equipment. Get her hooked up to an EKG machine so we can see if she has a heartbeat. And someone get an IV started so we can give her some meds." That, I could do.

I'd probably started hundreds of IVs by that point in my training and I was considered one of the best. I went right for the inside of her ankle—the "intern's vein," as we all called it. A nice, big juicy vein sat just above the inner ankle bone and we pediatricians usually went for that first, especially if the patient wasn't walking yet. I picked the biggest catheter I could find, but this was the infant ward after all, and the biggest catheter on our ward was tiny for an adult patient. Still, it was better than nothing, and I got that wonderful glow of success when I slipped it in on the first try.

Now that we had intravenous access, Larry started ordering Code medications. "Let's give her a dose of epi first," he ordered, and then he paused. What *was* the epinephrine dose in an adult patient? We all knew the doses of pediatric medications by heart, especially the emergency ones. But an adult? Luckily, there was a medical student present, and he'd just finished a rotation in the adult Emergency Department. "I think it's a cc of epi," he said, but we could tell he wasn't sure. Larry pondered this briefly and then decided to go ahead with that dose. Would it do any harm if we overshot the mark? Later on, we all admitted that we didn't think that anything we did would really make a difference. None of us had ever seen an adult survive a Code. Babies, on the other hand, often "came back," which sometimes left us wondering whether we'd done the right thing. After all, we'd muse, there are things worse than death.

By this time, we had our adult patient hooked up to our baby EKG machine. Larry stopped CPR again briefly, but her heartbeat was still "flatline" on the screen. "Another epi," he ordered, "and then a dose of calcium and bicarb." It was about this time that I suddenly became aware of Hannah. Her crib was just a few feet from all of us. She was wearing her little red pj's and she had pulled herself up to a stand, holding onto the side rail. She stood there, gazing intently at the chaotic scene in front of her. And then she began swaying back and forth, saying one of her favorite words, "uh-oh." Over and over again, she kept saying "uh-oh" as we struggled to save this woman.

One of the nurses who wasn't directly involved in the Code went over to Hannah, picked her up, and pushing her IV pole ahead of her, took her out of the room to the nearby nurses' station.

It had been only 20 minutes since we'd first heard the Code paged overhead, but it seemed like hours. We just weren't getting anywhere, and our meds didn't seem to be making any difference. Where was the adult Code team? We continued to hear the Code being paged, but we found out later that the adult team kept ignoring it because after all, the Code was on the infant ward, and why would they be needed there? Finally, though, the paging operator added the words "adult medicine" to the page and the adult team got the message. They burst in the door with an adult Code cart about 30 minutes after we baby doctors had arrived on the scene. For a moment, they were as stunned as we had been initially. They silently took in the mouth-to-mouth resuscitation, the tiny EKG leads and baby heart monitor, the small Code cart (with the pediatric medications on it), and—finally—my little IV in the woman's foot. "Is that all you could get in?" the senior resident asked. No one answered, but everyone looked at me, kneeling by her foot and turning a few shades of red. And I had been so proud of myself!

The adult team quickly recovered from the shock of our pathetic (to them) resuscitation attempts and went to work. They intubated the woman and began ventilating her with an adult bag. Then they put her on an adult heart monitor and we were all thrilled to see that there actually was a heartbeat, albeit way too slow. And they put a huge intravenous catheter into her femoral vein. More medications were ordered, and we could all see her heart rate slowly pick up until it became normal.

"We need a dose of Pronestyl," the senior resident ordered. This was an adult heart medication. But one of our nurses misunderstood and ran and got a bag of Pregestamil, which was Hannah's special baby formula. The adult Code team just busted up laughing, and we halfheartedly joined in. But everyone knew the joke was on us and inwardly, we were all seething. After all, we'd done the best we could under the circumstances and the patient had miraculously survived, at least for the short term. We felt proud of ourselves, and yet we knew that we were being mocked by the adult Code team and that they would be telling stories for a long time about what we had done—especially that itty-bitty IV in her foot vein.

As things were winding down, a distraught man and woman rushed into the room whom I recognized as Hannah's parents. They had come for their daily visit and saw all the commotion and equipment outside of Hannah's room, and they feared the worst. Then they saw her empty crib and her mother became hysterical. "Is she gone?" her father quietly asked. They didn't notice the elderly woman lying on the floor, hooked up to all sorts of equipment; all they could see was Hannah's empty crib.

I quickly went over to them and told them, over and over again, "It's not Hannah. She's fine. It's not her."

As I guided them from the room to the hallway to look for the nurse who had spirited Hannah away, I explained that an elderly visitor had had an apparent heart attack and that we had done everything we could to try to save her. I don't think they heard a word I was saying. They just wanted to see their baby girl and to know that she really was all right. Earlier on in her life, her parents had been awakened in the middle of the night by one of us residents, informing them that Hannah had "Coded." She'd been saved, but I remember thinking at the time, for what? So she could live the rest of her life in the hospital, hooked up to IV nutrition and unable to enjoy the taste of milk or rice cereal or ice cream? But now, as I saw her parents reunite with her at the nurses' station, I was overwhelmed by not only *their* incredible bond with *her*, but *her* bond with *them*. She had stopped saying "uh-oh" by now and was happily babbling "Mama" and "Dada," blowing raspberries and clapping her hands. Maybe someday they'll be able to do intestinal transplants on these kids, I thought to myself.

When I walked back into Hannah's room, I realized that the show was over. The adult team had already transported their patient to the medical intensive care unit, taking their Code cart and equipment with them. All that was left was the usual post-Code paraphernalia, strewn about the floor and on one of the empty incubators. This included little medication bottles, empty syringes, the occasional needle, pieces of packaging and paper—some of which contained written Code notes ("stout elderly woman," "no pulse," "CPR × 25 minutes," "IV inserted left foot—Dr. Gleason"). There I was, my accomplishment noted on a piece of paper towel that was sitting on top of the empty Isolette.

Our coffee-break time was long gone, having been used up by the unexpected Code. So we all scattered about the ward and began our daily tasks—which were even more daunting since it had been nearly two hours since we'd finished rounds. As I crossed off the third item on my prioritized "to do" list, it suddenly occurred to me that none of us knew who that woman was. And worse, none of us had even taken the time to try to find out. She must have been visiting someone in that room. The room had only four patients in it, and Hannah was one of them. I knew her parents had already been in, and so the woman couldn't be related to them, leaving three patients' families to consider. I knew that one of the babies in the room rarely had visitors because her parents were both in jail.

Her only visitors were from Child Protective Services, the agency that would eventually determine where she would go once she was discharged.

I went back out to the nurses' station and asked the head nurse if she had any information on the woman we had just resuscitated. She, too, had no clue. The woman had apparently walked into the room without stopping at the nurses' station first. That meant she must have visited before, or she wouldn't have known where to go. Although the babies' names were posted at the entrance to each room, there were 10 rooms on that ward and it would have taken awhile for someone to have checked all 10 entrances, looking for one particular name.

"Didn't anyone see her before she collapsed?" I asked. "Who called the Code?" The head nurse explained that no one except the babies were in the room at the time. We doctors were all in the cafeteria, and the nurses had finished their morning assessments and were gathered at the nurses' station. That's when they heard a heavy thud coming from Hannah's room and ran to investigate. This was turning out to be a bit of a mystery, right here on our unit.

I went back into Hannah's room and saw her parents there, playing with her as she sat in her favorite infant swing. They both looked up at me and simultaneously said, "So how's she doing?" I told them what I'd told them before—that we'd done the best we could and at least for the time being, it seemed as though we'd been successful. I added that the woman had been taken to the adult ICU and that I hoped we'd find out more later. They went back to playing with Hannah, and when I asked them whether they were planning to stay for the whole day, they told me that they were having a formal Christmas picture taken and were waiting for the photographer, a Mrs. Grady, to arrive.

I paused.

"Did you know Mrs. Grady?" I asked. "Had you ever met

with her before?" No, they explained, they had simply gone with a recommendation from a friend of theirs who'd done something similar when their baby boy was hospitalized for several weeks before Christmas. And then we all looked at each other, each of us thinking the same thing.

I ran back to the nurses' station and called the Medical Intensive Care Unit (MICU); such weird though similar acronyms, I thought. Our unit was the NICU; the adult medical unit was the MICU. Then there was the Surgical ICU (SICU) and the Pediatric ICU (PICU).

When the MICU receptionist answered the phone, I introduced myself as one of the "baby doctors" who had been involved in the recent adult Code on the infant floor. My heart sank as she laughed and said, "Yes, they're all talking about it." And this was just the unit clerk.

I then asked her whether she knew the patient's identity, as we wanted to prepare the family if she was related to one of our babies.

"We do know her name. It's Genevieve Grady," she said. "And if you ask me, it looks like she might be some kind of a photographer, possibly on some sort of hospital assignment. She had a camera bag with her with several rolls of film in it, and she had a slip of paper in her pocket with a patient name and room number on it."

I thanked her for the information and confirmed her hunch. She told me that from her vantage point, it looked like it was touch and go, but then, she wasn't really supposed to give me any information. I should just come by and talk to the doctors if I wanted the real scoop. I would do that later. Now, I just wanted to let Hannah's parents know that their Christmas picture was off, and why.

At first, they were genuinely shocked. And then, somehow, they felt guilty, and so did I. We had, each in our own way, been so relieved that the Code wasn't being run on Hannah that we hadn't even stopped to question who was being Coded. Such an odd use of the language, that word "Code," used as both a noun and a verb. It was the same with the term "DNR" (do not resuscitate). When parents made that decision about their dying baby, the directive DNR turned into a description of the baby on rounds. "She's a DNR now," we'd remind each other. That meant nobody would "Code" her if she "arrested" (her heart stopped).

That "adult" Code, as we pediatric residents referred to it, was the chief topic of conversation at our after-rounds coffee-and-doughnut sessions for the next few days. We retold all the funny stories (including of course my tiny foot IV), and we marveled that we had somehow "gotten her back."

We stopped talking about it, though, when we found out that the woman had never regained consciousness. After several days that must have been agonizing for her family, support was discontinued and she was allowed to die a dignified death in the arms of her husband. How similar that sounded to us! Whenever we had the chance, we, too, tried to "orchestrate death" when parents were ready to accept the inevitable.

But somehow, death from a massive heart attack at the end of a long and, one hopes, satisfying life seemed so much easier to live with than Hannah's death. Two weeks after Mrs. Grady's life support was withdrawn, Hannah developed a high fever and just lay down in her crib. She never stood up again; never held her arms out to her favorite nurses; never again said "uh-oh." She'd become septic, for the tenth and last time, from her central IV — her lifeline — and it was time to say good-bye. In some ways, it seemed almost as hard for me to let her go as it was for her parents, but of course, my sense of loss paled in comparison to theirs, and to that of the nurses who'd cared for her all her life. After all, I was only on the ward for a one-month rotation. Her parents and the staff nurses on the floor had loved and cared for her for a whole year.

And then I thought of Mrs. Grady's family, some of whom, like her husband, had loved and cherished her for 50 years or more. Death is never easy for the living.

CHAPTER 7

Roxie

I GRADUATED FROM medical school on May 26, 1979 — as a very new bride. The day before, I'd married one of my medical school classmates. We were the only couple at our graduation ceremony who had both met and married during medical school — and the first that anyone knew of who had married each other the day before graduation. It was not an auspicious beginning, as it turned out.

We'd met during the first week of classes, although I really don't recall the exact moment. What I do remember is spending one night together getting to know each other — and not realizing how long we'd been talking until dawn broke. We were pretty much a couple after that night and sometime during our second or third year, we moved in together — into a four-bedroom house near the medical school that his father had bought for $23,000 as an investment. It felt like playing house for the entire time that we lived there.

Of the two of us, he was the intellectual one. He was a much better classroom student than I was, at least in the first two preclinical years, when we spent most of our time attending lectures and labs and taking exams. He really excelled in that setting, getting A's or honors in nearly everything. I, on the other hand, had struggled with the required math and science courses all through college, and so it came as no surprise to me that anatomy, physiology, biochemistry, genetics, and pharmacology were equally challenging. I was happy with a C or a Pass grade and received only one honors grade—for Introduction to Clinical Care. But the balance shifted when we began our clinical rotations in the third year. Learning to take care of real patients was the reason I went to medical school. Although there were still clinical exams to pass, now the material I read and studied seemed more relevant. These were real people with real diseases, and I was excited to learn all I could about them. It just "stuck" better than memorizing all the muscles of the arm or the biochemical pathway for glucose production.

I didn't decide to become a pediatrician until the fall of my senior year of medical school, when I'd scheduled my last clinical rotation, which was pediatrics. I'd scheduled it last because I was sure that I would never choose to specialize in that field. Even though I'd had a lot of personal experience with kids, having two younger sisters and a baby brother, I'd had one very bad babysitting experience that convinced me that I would never be good with kids. I hadn't done much babysitting, but for some reason I said yes when I was asked to sit for two neighborhood boys, ages seven and nine. They seemed like pretty normal kids while their mother gave me the rundown on their evening schedule, but as soon as their parents walked out the door, those boys went wild. They started jumping up and down on the living room furniture and throwing cushions and pillows at me, disregarding everything I tried to do or say to distract them or to make them stop.

After what seemed like hours of this behavior I told them they needed to go to bed, and that whipped them up into even more of a frenzy. I just didn't know what to do and so finally, I broke down and called my father for help. He came right over and within five minutes, he had those kids upstairs and in their beds. I felt incompetent, humiliated, and convinced that I would henceforth never do anything that involved taking care of children.

So when I finally decided to become a doctor, I'd naturally assumed that the *last* kind of doctor I'd want to become was a pediatrician. But amazingly, I loved it from the moment I set foot on the pediatric wards. Partly, it was because of the people who'd chosen to work there. Pediatric nurses and doctors are generally just nice people, and they like to have fun. Everyone wore little stuffed creatures on their stethoscopes, and the nurses usually wore colorful, playful scrubs instead of the standard hospital-issue blues.

And it was also the kids. They were so incredibly resilient, and most did well—so unlike the patients on the adult medical wards, which were filled with elderly people whose bodies were giving out, often because they hadn't taken good care of themselves—having subjected their bodies to smoking, excessive drinking, obesity, et cetera. With kids, bad things just happened to them; they didn't bring it on themselves. And most of the time, we could fix them up and get them back to being kids again. Even the very sickest of kids would somehow be able to play and squeeze some joy out of a seemingly joyless situation.

My future husband had decided to become an internist. He knew he didn't want to be a private practice doctor, but rather an academic physician with a faculty appointment and time to do research and teach. Although I was sure about pediatrics, I was undecided as to private practice or academic medicine. This became somewhat of a problem as we prepared to hit the road, interviewing for internship positions—as a couple.

A computerized ranking system, fondly called "the Match," had been established to help both internship applicants and programs to match their top choices. You visited programs in your chosen specialty, and then you submitted your top residency program choices on a specified date. Likewise, each residency program prepared a list of its top-ranked candidates. When the two lists "matched," you were assigned to that program. Couples were allowed to "Couples Match," which meant that they submitted the same list and could match only if both of them matched to that program. So we needed to find places that had both good academic internal medicine programs and strong, broad-based pediatrics programs. And both programs would have to rank us pretty highly. Occasionally, things were arranged "outside the Match," which relieved loads of anxiety on the part of the applicants and involved both program directors from the same institution getting together and saying "we'll take her if you take him" or vice versa.

We drove my grandmother's orange Dodge Dart Swinger up and down the East Coast, visiting programs in New York, Florida, North Carolina, Washington, D.C., Michigan, and Cleveland. It was a grueling three-week trip and at the end of it, we of course liked different programs. Making a Couples Match list wasn't going to be easy. But a few weeks after we returned, we received a call from Case Western Reserve University Hospitals in Cleveland. Both the internal medicine and pediatric residency program directors were prepared to offer us positions, outside the Match. Cleveland was not a top choice for either one of us, but we hadn't categorically ruled out its programs either, so after thinking it over for one night, we decided to accept. We were actually going to be residents! In Cleveland, Ohio, of all places, but still, we were going to be residents. Who cared that people called the city "the mistake on the lake" and that the Cuyahoga River had recently caught fire?

Two weeks later, we became engaged. Now, not only were we going to be residents, we were going to be *married* residents. We decided to get married the day before graduation in part to make it easier for our families and friends to double up both occasions, and in part because of how our relationship had evolved. We'd met at the beginning of medical school and we would get married at the end.

After a brief honeymoon on Hilton Head Island, we moved to Cleveland to start our residencies. I'd been anticipating July 1 for so long that it was a let down when I got my schedule during orientation and realized that my very first rotation was in the emergency room, and I wasn't scheduled to be there until July 2. While my new husband set off on July 1 for his first ward rotation as a *doctor* (albeit a green one), I spent the whole day reading books about pediatric emergencies, trying to prepare myself for what lay ahead.

Once I actually got started, the first year went by in an incredibly intense blur. At times, it seemed impossible to visualize actually finishing the year, making it through alive and somewhat intact. We were on call either every other night or every third night throughout the year—and we had only two weeks' vacation. We were able to schedule that vacation at the same time, through a stroke of luck. We bought ourselves a pair of unlimited-mileage airline tickets and traveled all over the country, staying with family and friends. It was a nice trip, but not exactly relaxing. I would have been just as happy to stay home for the entire two weeks, just sleeping in, reading, cooking, and taking long walks. But we were different in that way and in many others.

We did enjoy one new nonmedical experience together during that internship year, and that was Major League Baseball. I'd never been to a baseball game before, but even though the Cleveland Indians were perpetually in the cellar of their league, we residents found the games to be a cheap and fun diversion. We'd scrounge up tickets to the home games, usually cheap bleacher seats, and those of us who weren't on call would take the Rapid Transit trains to the old stadium and cheer on our loser heroes. It was so nice to get away from the hospital for such a mindless game.

I really got into it, joining the "Hargrove's Howlers," which was first baseman Mike Hargrove's fan club. We'd try to sit in line with his first-base position so we could watch all his moves from the rear. I was so excited when I found out that the All Star Game would be in Cleveland that summer! Several of us were lucky enough to get tickets. Then it happened—the first Major League Baseball strike. And although it was finally resolved in time for the All Star Game, the magic had gone out of the game for me; I quit being a fan and gave away my All Star tickets. I realized that baseball was really just a business, and fans like me were marketed just like all other customers.

We both became second-year residents on July 1, 1980, and although the residency program remained just as intense, at least we weren't interns anymore—that lowly rung on the academic medicine ladder. By that time, I had already made the decision that I would become a neonatologist—one of the few decisions I've made in my life on which I've never wavered. My husband hadn't really decided yet, but he was still committed to an academic career and so he knew he would need to specialize further. I had become quite close to the other interns in my residency "class," and so had he. It was hard not to—you worked so intensely together and saw each other almost every day. There was only one affiliated hospital besides the "mother ship," and we rotated there for only one month each year. Of course, I knew his colleagues and he knew mine, but we rarely socialized together because our call schedules rarely coincided.

This, as it turns out, did not bode well for our marriage. He began spending more and more time with Ellen, one of the other residents in his training program. I knew they were good friends but I didn't realize how good—even when he went to a party at Ellen's one night and didn't come home until the next morning. The truth is, I was so busy at work, and we had so little time together, that I was oblivious to what might have been going on.

So it came as a genuine shock to me when one day we were both off for the evening and he said he wanted to go for a walk. And on that walk, he told me that he didn't want to be married anymore. He insisted that there wasn't anyone else; he just didn't want to be married. He'd already started looking for his own apartment and was planning to move out as soon as he found one. He hoped I would understand. After all, these things happened all the time.

But I couldn't believe this was happening to me. I wish I could say that I remained calm and strong in the face of adversity, but although that came later, at the time I was anything but. I cried; I begged him not to do this; I asked him "why?" over and over again. I felt as though I were in a dream and that when I awoke, I'd be so relieved that it hadn't really happened. But it did happen, and after a terrible, sleepless night, I had to go back to the hospital and continue my PICU rotation as though nothing had occurred.

It turned out to be a relief and a distraction, plunging into the daily grind of morning rounds and then the typically long "to do" list on my patients in the unit. One of those patients was a four-year-old girl named Roxie who'd gotten chicken pox and then, just as she was getting over the worst of the fever and scratching, started vomiting and acting "like a zombie," as her mother described it. This had rapidly progressed to a coma and she was rushed to the hospital, where blood tests revealed a high ammonia level and liver inflammation, which led to the diagnosis of that mysterious disease called Reye's syndrome. We didn't know much about it in those days (the link to aspirin hadn't been discovered yet), and all we could do was provide life support and wait for the ammonia level to come down, the liver to "cool off," and the pressure in the brain to decrease. If that happened, the child would gradually "wake up," and then we'd find out how much brain damage there was. And if that didn't happen, the child would die.

Roxie had an interesting twist to her Reye's that made her care even more challenging. Patients with Reye's usually needed a lot of extra glucose (sugar) because their inflamed liver couldn't release it from its glucose storage depot or make it *de novo*, as the liver normally does. So these patients would quickly become hypoglycemic if something happened to their IV or if we didn't put enough glucose into their IV fluid. But Roxie was the exact opposite. When she'd been admitted to the PICU two days before, her blood sugar had been in the normal range, which in retrospect should have been a red flag for the sugar problems she would later develop. As I finished up my standard, "problem-oriented" presentation of her case on morning rounds, the PICU fellow paused for a moment and then asked me how much glucose she was requiring in her IV fluid. He caught me off guard, because although I'd informed the team exactly what was in her IV fluid and what the infusion rate was, I hadn't done the math to determine exactly how much glucose that infusion gave her.

"I haven't done the calculations," I admitted to the PICU fellow, who was standing at the foot of her bed. "But I think she's needing less than usual, because she's only on D5." This meant that her IV solution was only 5 percent dextrose (or glucose), and typically these children needed at least 10 percent dextrose.

"You should be doing a glucose index every day on these patients, Chris," he admonished. "Well, could you at least tell us what her last blood sugar was?"

"Let's see," I replied, and I felt my face flush the way it always did when I was embarrassed or had done something wrong. We residents were supposed to collect all the data on our patients before rounds started. I should have known and already reported what her blood sugar was. I quickly scanned the bedside flow chart maintained by the nurses. "Her blood sugar this morning was 150," I finally reported to the impatient team.

"So she's needing about half the sugar of other Reye's patients and still, her blood sugar is about twice as high. Have you thought about what's going on here, Chris?"

Actually, I hadn't. I prided myself on knowing every detail about my patients, more than the senior residents and ICU fellows. How had I missed this? Had I just been too preoccupied with my own personal crisis? I felt tears start to well up in my eyes, which had never, *ever* happened before in my professional life. I just couldn't cry on rounds. I quickly grabbed a tissue from Roxie's bedside table and muttered something about a contact lens attack.

"Have you ever heard of diabetes?" he asked, somewhat sarcastically, as I kept dabbing at my eyes.

Of course I had, but because I hadn't paid attention to her blood sugar level or her glucose requirements, it hadn't occurred to me that her pancreas could be functioning abnormally. This might mean that she could actually have diabetes, which had gone undetected until she got sick, or that the Reye's had affected her pancreas—perhaps transiently. In either case, the fellow explained, as I nodded numbly, we'd need to treat her similarly. And that might mean she'd need insulin if her blood sugar climbed much higher or she developed more acid and ketones in her blood.

I'd already learned how to treat kids who came into the emergency room with their first presentation of diabetes, which was called diabetic ketoacidosis, so I was familiar with the management plan the fellow was outlining. But I tried to listen respectfully as he instructed me to check Roxie's blood sugar and acid level throughout the day and night (I was on call that night), and to start an insulin drip if her blood sugar went higher than 200 or if she started to have more acid in her blood. The tricky part was to be careful not to increase her IV fluid infusion rate in the process, because that could cause more problems for her already swollen brain.

I was so relieved when we moved on to the next patient, a little toddler with meningitis who belonged to the other resident working with me in the PICU. When rounds were finally over, I went into busy PICU resident mode, moving through my long "to do" list, which included ordering blood sugars and blood gases to be drawn every four hours on Roxie. While my husband's declaration lingered in the back of my mind, it was like a canker sore that hurts only when you touch it with your tongue or eat something like chocolate.

I had a break around dinnertime and so I was glad when one of my fellow residents, Susan, came to see if I could have dinner with her. The PICU fellow was still in the unit, and he said he'd stay until I got back. Susan and I went down to the cafeteria. By this time, well into our second year of residency training, we were all a very close-knit group, brought together primarily by our common struggle to get through this grueling experience intact.

As we wolfed down hamburgers, Susan started telling me about her latest love. I don't know how she managed to find the time and energy for dating, but somehow she did. She'd had several relationships since starting her residency and I usually enjoyed hearing about them. But that evening I didn't, and it must have showed. Susan asked me what was wrong, and before I had a chance to think about whether I wanted to keep this to myself or not, the whole, sad story came pouring out.

"I'm not surprised," she said when I'd finished.

Suddenly it dawned on me that maybe there *was* someone else, and maybe that someone was Ellen. Right then and there, in the hospital cafeteria, I felt myself morph from shock and disbelief into anger and steely resolve. Within 10 minutes (we both had to get back to our units), Susan helped me to devise a plan that would both sustain me and show everyone what I was made of.

My husband had told me that for weeks he'd been planning to move out, taking his share of our belongings with him. But I decided that *I* would be the one to move, leaving him to deal with the furniture and memorabilia I would leave behind. And amazingly enough, there was suddenly a place for me to move to. Susan told me that John, her new boyfriend, had asked her to move in with him, and now she had another reason to say yes. I could sublet her apartment while I looked for my own place, and I could move in the next day. John had a pickup truck and could help me pack up and move my stuff.

I headed back to the PICU feeling strangely buoyed. I had a plan. I was going to begin a new life in my own place, on my own terms.

A new patient was on the way up from the ER, the PICU fellow informed me when I returned. It was the first of three admissions I would get that night and each one required arterial and central venous lines to be placed, and lots of orders. I didn't get around to checking Roxie's blood sugars until 4 A.M., when the new admissions were finally "tucked in." I saw that her midnight blood sugar had climbed to 225 and her blood pH had fallen to 7.3, lower than the 7.35 it had been on morning rounds. It was time to start her on an insulin drip. I calculated how much insulin needed to be added to the bag of fluid and what drip rate the nurses should begin. Since her blood sugar wasn't sky high, I started her on a low dose of insulin, planning to titrate the drip rate to her blood sugars, which would now need to be drawn every 30 minutes. I wrote the orders, being careful to adjust her other fluids so that she wouldn't be getting any more than she was already receiving, and notified her nurse. Then, I went to the on-call room to lie down for an hour or so before I had to get up to collect all that patient data needed for morning rounds.

As was typically the case when I tried to sleep when I was on call, I couldn't get to sleep at first. My beeper was on the bedside table, and I knew it could go off at any time. And because the on-call room was just off the unit, I could hear the beeps of the monitors and the voices of the unit staff. No crying, though. Most of the kids in the unit were on ventilators, so it was strangely quiet compared to the regular children's ward.

I started thinking about my plan to move into Susan's apartment, and a combination of excitement, nervousness, and depression started lulling me into a kind of half-sleep.

Suddenly, I sat bolt upright in the bed. "Oh my God!" I cried aloud, to no one but myself. I'd suddenly realized that I'd made an error on Roxie's insulin drip. I'd had the same feeling you get when you suddenly realize you left the front door unlocked, just after your flight takes off for a month-long vacation. I don't know how or why the brain does that. But it does.

I leapt out of bed and raced over to Roxie's bedside, where the nurse was just hanging the insulin drip. My heart was pounding.

"Wait!" I shouted to her. "Don't hang that drip! I need to double-check the order." And when I did, I realized that I really had made an error: I'd written 10 times the insulin dose I'd intended to start her on. She would have become hypoglycemic and we wouldn't have known, because she was already in a coma. And her brain could have been even more injured than it already was from the Reye's syndrome.

Relief flooded through me as I realized that nothing terrible had happened because of my error. I had picked it up in time. But then, as I sat at the nurses' station with a cup of coffee—there was no way I could sleep now—I wondered if I'd made the error because I'd been so distracted. Would I be able to function safely and effectively as a resident while I dealt with my own personal crisis? Would I know if I was "losing it"? Maybe I needed someone to watch over me and make sure I didn't screw up while I sorted out my life.

After rounds that morning, I went directly to our chief resident's office and told Alan the whole story, including the almost fatal error I'd made earlier that morning. When I'd finished, I asked him to please let me know if he saw any indication that my work was suffering in some way. And if he did, I told him, I was prepared to take a leave from my residency program.

Alan looked at me for a moment. He was normally a very funny guy, but this time he didn't crack any jokes.

"Chris," he said quietly, "I know you'd never let your personal problems get in the way of patient care. You know yourself better than I do and you'd know if you were 'losing it.' But I'm glad you told me what's going on so I can help you if you need it, including giving you some leave time. Now as for that insulin drip, we all make mistakes. The important thing, especially in medicine, is to learn from them so you never make the same mistake twice. And it shouldn't just be *you* learning from the mistake: it should be everyone involved in the care of that patient. Why didn't the pharmacy question your order? Why didn't the nurse double-check the drip calculation against what you'd verbally told her? I want you to participate in something new we're starting on the pediatric units: a 'root cause analysis' in which we assemble a whole team to review every aspect of a 'near miss' like this. The purpose is not to point fingers or to blame anyone, but to make sure it doesn't happen again."

This type of error review turned out to be way ahead of its time. Today, preventing medical errors is, fortunately, a major focus of all hospitals, but back then, this was a novel approach. And I was so relieved both to unburden myself about it and to participate in some way in making sure that neither I nor anyone else hurt a patient by making the same error.

I left the hospital around noon and went home. The apartment looked, smelled, and felt different somehow. I quickly packed up my things—there really wasn't much—and then John and Susan arrived with John's pickup truck. We piled everything, including my beloved desk, into the truck and drove it to Susan's apartment. It took only an hour to unpack it all, and then John drove me back to the house so I could get my car. I took a last look around and decided to leave my soon-to-be ex-husband a note.

Then, for some reason, I found myself standing by the fireplace with our bride-and-groom champagne glasses in my hands and I did something that felt SO good. I hurled those glasses against the fireplace, smashing them to pieces. After savoring the moment, I looked down at the broken glass scattered everywhere, even on the hearth, and I suddenly had a vision of my husband accidentally stepping on a piece of it, cutting an artery in his foot, and slowly bleeding to death. And so I took a broom and swept up all that glass into the fireplace.

From that day on, I decided to keep moving forward and strengthen my inner resolve to make it through this as a better, stronger person. It was the worst thing that had ever happened to me, but I knew that so many other people had endured far, far worse.

Back in the PICU the next day, I was delighted to find that Roxie's blood sugar and ammonia levels were both down. The insulin drip I'd written (the correct one) had been needed for only about 12 hours and it turned out in the end that her diabetes had only been transient, an unusual complication of her Reye's syndrome. She was also one of those more fortunate kids who, when fully recovered from her Reye's, didn't have any brain damage. She was able to come off the respirator the next day, and suddenly she became a real kid—kicking and screaming and wailing for her mother. She was transferred to the children's ward the next day, and went home soon after. I happened to be there a year later when her parents brought her back to the PICU, bearing a huge basket of delightful junk food for the staff. Roxie herself handed out pieces of candy and bags of chips, saying "thank you" to each of the recipients.

She was a kindergarten star, her parents proudly proclaimed to the gathered staff.

But I kept thinking about how awful it would have been if she'd been brain damaged because of my insulin drip error. I presented the case to the new quality improvement team, as Alan had asked me to do, and was relieved that no one asked me why I'd made such a stupid mistake. Most of the team's questions were centered on why no one along the way had questioned or even double-checked the order I'd written. A new process was created for all insulin drips on the pediatric units that we all hoped would prevent similar calculation errors.

As for my personal resolve, I called one of those law offices advertised on TV. The firm said it could handle a simple divorce for about $250, so I signed on. I found a fabulous apartment in an old mansion near the hospital. Finally, I decided that I would become the best pediatric resident in my class by pouring myself into my work. I did a clinical research project with one of the faculty neonatologists, which I presented at a national research meeting in Washington, D.C. The abstract was expanded to become my very first published research paper—"The Optimal Position for Spinal Tap in Preterm Infants"—and sparked my interest in academic medicine. I spent lots of time developing teaching tools for the interns and medical students and as a result, I received the Outstanding Resident Teaching Award.

Just before I finished my residency training, I decided to use my one remaining week of vacation to go to a country inn near my parents' summer home in Canandaigua, New York, on a package deal described as a "Sojourn for the Spirit." During that week of solitude, I fasted for a day (for the first and last time) and watched what has now become my favorite old movie—*Same Time, Next Year,* starring Alan Alda and Ellen Burstyn. Ironically, they fall in love at a chance meeting at a Mendocino inn, and although they're both married, they develop a deep, lasting relationship based upon their once-a-year rendezvous at the same time, same place.

I wrote a paper on the use of vitamin E in premature infants, which won a prize at the pediatric department's Research Day. And I applied for neonatology fellowships and wound up being accepted at my first choice, in San Francisco. There, I worked under the tutelage of Dr. Roberta Ballard, an incredible mentor who has now become a dear friend. I also met a man named Erik on a blind date. On our second date, sitting at the Washington Square Bar and Grill, sipping Manhattans, I gave him a line that I'd read in *Good Housekeeping* magazine, of all places.

"You remind me of my…*second* husband," I said slowly, to which he obligingly replied, sounding surprised, "How many times have you been married?" which nicely allowed me to deliver the punchline: "Once."

And later, he did become my second husband, the father of my children, and the real love of my life.

CHAPTER 8

Emily

IT WAS JULY 1, and across the country newly minted doctors, fresh from medical school, were beginning their residency training—all on the same day. "Whatever you do, don't get sick or have an accident on July first" was often said, somewhat jokingly, by hospital staff everywhere. For some residency graduates like me, the next stage of our training also began on July 1. In my case, this was the first day of my three-year fellowship in neonatology. I was nervous, but it was nothing compared to my first day of pediatric internship. I spent the day being oriented to the training program and to the NICU, where I would do most of my advanced clinical work. Clinical training would not actually take up the majority of my time, as was the case in my pediatric residency program; I would also be learning how to do basic laboratory research from a master physician-scientist at an affiliated university research institute.

In order to be able to take the neonatology board exams at the end of my training, I would need to demonstrate "meaningful accomplishment in research." I was more nervous about this—a completely new venture for me—than I was about my increasing level of clinical responsibility in the NICU. After all, as a pediatric resident, I'd spent a total of eight months working in the NICU, and I felt pretty experienced. But the last time I'd been in a research lab was during a college biology course in which I'd done some sort of experiments with rats and their kidneys. I knew that in a lab, I'd feel like a fish out of water compared to the familiar hospital environment. Still, when I found out that I was going to be on call that first night, covering the NICU "in house" with a couple of pediatric residents, I developed a typical case of "the dreads." This was what I called the butterflies in my stomach and general apprehension I always got—and still get—when beginning a new clinical service rotation.

Shortly after I received "sign-out"—concise information about each of the babies in the NICU—I was called to the delivery room for "thick mec." "Mec" was short for meconium (Greek for "poppy juice"), the green, sticky first stool of a newborn baby. Sometimes, particularly when the pregnancy went past the due date, a stressed-out fetus would pass meconium into the amniotic sac before birth. This could create a problem when the baby took the first breath and inhaled some of this meconium into the lungs. So, the obstetrician would call the pediatrician or neonatologist (or fellow, in my case) to "suck mec" immediately after birth; in other words, to intubate and apply suction in order to remove any meconium *before* the baby took the first breath.

The hospital where I was doing all my clinical training had an alternative birth center (ABC). In the ABC, mothers could deliver their babies in an environment that was as close to home as possible. This was before the days when all hospital delivery rooms looked more like rooms from a five-star hotel, with parquet floors, normal beds with comforters, Jacuzzi tubs in the bathroom, and all the medical equipment hidden away in cabinets from which it could be pulled out in an instant, when needed. In the ABC, all rooms looked like that and mothers could turn down the lights, play their own music, use aromatherapy—in the three years I was there, I think I saw it all. But there were certain conditions under which mothers were required to move to the regular delivery rooms because the delivery was not expected to be completely normal, and thick mec was one of those conditions.

So, when I was called for thick mec, I went with the pediatric resident I'd be supervising straight to one of the delivery rooms. There, one of the ABC moms was already pushing to get the baby out. I could tell it was an ABC mom because the lights were low, soft music was playing in the background, and various oils were being used to ease the baby's head out.

We quickly prepared the equipment we'd need to suction the baby's trachea and resuscitate the baby, if needed afterward. I quickly scanned the mother's chart, finding that she was an "elderly primip" (first pregnancy; age over 35) and that her only problem during the pregnancy had been some mildly elevated blood pressures. She'd had genetic testing because of her age (which increased the chance of a chromosome problem such as Down syndrome), and she and her husband had been relieved to find that they were having a girl—with a normal 46XX karyotype. Her due date was the week before, putting her at 41 weeks' gestation. She was Vietnamese and had moved to the United States only two years earlier.

And then I read something that gave me pause. Her husband was a newly minted doctor who was beginning his residency at the big university hospital. This was a little too close for comfort. I found out later that he'd met his wife-to-be when he'd spent a summer in Vietnam during medical school, working in a rural health clinic. They'd hoped that by the time July 1 rolled around, they'd already have had the baby and perhaps a week to adjust to life as parents. But the timing of birth and babies was rarely convenient, in my limited experience anyway.

So on the day the father-to-be was to begin his residency, the mother-to-be had begun her labor. I spoke briefly to the parents, who wanted to know how soon they'd be able to hold their baby. I assured them that we'd be "sucking mec" as quickly after birth as possible. If the baby didn't need more attention after we were finished, we'd bring her right over. Since they knew from the genetic testing that their baby was a girl, they told me they'd already named her Emily. The father was most concerned that nothing interfere with their ability to bond with Emily. He'd had a very difficult time trying to explain to his laboring wife why they'd had to leave the ABC and come to this relatively sterile delivery room. I assured him that we'd work as quickly as we could to get our job done.

Suddenly, with a heavy grunt and a final push, there she was.

Emily didn't cry, which was good for us. I supervised the pediatric resident placing the tube in her trachea and helped her suction a small amount of meconium out. When it looked as though all was clear, the tube was removed and we began to stimulate the baby. Now, we *wanted* her to cry—she needed to expand her lungs and get on with the transition from being a fetus to being a newborn. It took a little longer than usual but then, there it was, that first, miraculous cry.

Except that Emily's cry didn't sound right to me, or to the midwife, who glanced over at me when she heard it. I took a closer look at the baby and discovered that one of her arms was significantly shorter than the other because part of her forearm was missing. It's funny how you don't notice those things at first, when you're concentrating on sucking meconium or getting the baby resuscitated. She was also smaller than usual. When we eventually put her on the scale, she weighed just over five pounds even though she was past her due date. She didn't seem to be having any breathing problems, but she wasn't pinking up in the way newborn babies generally do after the first few minutes of life. Her color was slightly bluish.

I began to realize that Emily likely had a syndrome. It wasn't going to be a typical chromosome abnormality, like Down syndrome, because fetal genetic testing had been normal. But there were thousands of syndromes in which the chromosomes were normal, at least in number, on fetal testing. Because nonchromosomal syndromes couldn't be diagnosed with a blood test (at least not in those days), it was important not to simply guess at the diagnosis, particularly in the newborn period. Of course, parents are desperate to know what's wrong with their child, and they'll hang onto your every word. But if you guess and your guess proves to be wrong (something usually revealed as the child grows), the parents can be devastated—and very often, angry. Still, when I saw Emily's face, I suddenly knew what syndrome she had. And it wasn't going to be a guess.

At first glance, there wasn't anything obviously wrong. But when I took a closer look, I saw that her facial features were somewhat coarse and her eyebrows met in the center of her forehead. I'd only seen pictures in textbooks, but I was suddenly sure that I was looking at the face of a baby with Cornelia de Lange, a very rare syndrome. A neonatologist might see only one in his or her entire career. Sadly, the developmental outcome was typically worse than for Down syndrome, with more severe mental retardation being the norm. Emily probably also had a serious congenital heart defect and might need surgery to survive.

I'd never seen a case before and a delicious thrill went through me as I realized that I'd not only recognized the key features, but I'd been able to put them together with the correct diagnosis. What an incredible start to my neonatology fellowship—a great case that *I'd* picked up in the delivery room! Just wait till my new colleagues (the three other fellows in my training program) heard about it. And then, the other reality of the situation hit me—her parents.

They were both looking at me, and I knew I needed to say something to them. I'd recognized unexpected birth defects in the delivery room before, and I'd had to break the news to parents who were eagerly anticipating their perfect "Gerber baby," as we called it. But this was different. The new dad had just started his residency and I was just starting my fellowship. It was suddenly so close to home.

At least Emily didn't need any more resuscitation, although I was still worried about her color. We'd been giving her some oxygen by mask, although if the problem was with her heart, as I suspected, the extra oxygen wouldn't do any good. But I used that as an excuse to explain to her parents why I wasn't able to bring her over to them to hold. And, as gently as I could, I told them about her shortened left arm and her unusual facial features. I told them that I suspected a syndrome, but I didn't say which one. We'd need to do further tests and arrange a consultation from a geneticist at the university. Her father looked at me before he began to translate for his wife. "It's bad, isn't it?" he said. I looked away, mumbling something to the effect of "let's wait and see."

After he spoke to his wife in fluent Vietnamese, he went over to the delivery room table with his camera, but he didn't take a picture. He just stared for a few minutes at his daughter and then asked me if it was okay for him to hold her, with the oxygen in place. It was, and he did. No one said a word. He carefully laid her back down and turned to me, shaking his head slowly back and forth and saying, "I don't know how I'm going to deal with this. I've just started my residency. What are we going to do?" It was gut-wrenching, hearing the helplessness and fear in his voice.

Over the next few days, we kept Emily in the NICU while we performed various tests and asked for consultations from the cardiologists and geneticists. The geneticists confirmed that she did indeed have Cornelia de Lange syndrome. There was praise for me for having recognized her features and made the diagnosis so quickly. And I have to admit that I was still thrilled with that—especially on my very first night on call as a fellow. I was confident in my diagnostic abilities already, but now, people meeting me for the first time would recognize that, too. I had begun to establish myself, and that was very important to me at the time. But inwardly, a battle was raging. I felt terribly guilty that the very "success" I'd had was, in a way, at the expense of this baby and her terribly distraught family.

I found it very difficult to relate to both of Emily's parents, for different reasons. With her mother, it was the language barrier and a growing sense among the unit staff that she didn't quite "get it"—that her daughter had a very disabling syndrome and that she would need intensive surgical and medical care in order to survive. There were clear cultural differences that our unit's social worker was trying to figure out in order to help the rest of us be able to relate to and work with Emily's mother. We were learning that in Vietnam, parents were more likely to accept whatever hand they were dealt, no matter how bad it was, and to "do everything" for their children. This just didn't feel right to some of the staff or to me—especially when I realized what the implications would be for her father.

With her father, it was of course the "too close to home" piece of the relationship. There was also a growing sense among the unit staff that in his case, he did "get it" and he was making it pretty clear that he didn't want it. He didn't want the disruption in his training and career; he didn't want to raise a severely disabled child; and he didn't want to put his daughter through surgery and painful procedures if the outcome was going to be bad anyway. While most of the staff (and me) tended to side with her father, it became increasingly uncomfortable to do so, particularly as we began to better realize and understand her mother's background. And some sort of decision had to be made soon—do we go ahead and "do everything"? Or do we just provide "comfort measures" and let Emily go?

Emily's heart defect was her "ticket out," a term we used to describe a way that she could die naturally. Her defect kept the well-oxygenated blood that returned from her lungs from getting to the rest of her body. We'd started her on intravenous prostaglandin, a medication that kept open the ductus arteriosus, a fetal blood vessel just outside the heart that connects the aorta to the pulmonary aorta. This blood vessel normally closes within 24 hours of birth, but in Emily's case, keeping it open was the only way to get oxygenated blood from her lungs to the rest of her body. Heart surgery was the only way to get her off the prostaglandin infusion. The surgeon could create a conduit just like the ductus, but that would only help her temporarily and would never completely fix the problem—she would need several more surgeries as she grew older.

Her parents agonized over what to do and we agonized with them. If she went through heart surgery now, she could come off the prostaglandins and go home. But what then? She'd need more operations as she grew, and she would likely be significantly handicapped. Even without a serious heart defect, children with Cornelia de Lange syndrome had a shortened life expectancy. Should she spend those years in and out of hospitals and the operating room?

Emily was about two weeks old when she began to have complications from the prostaglandin drip. The medication not only kept open the ductus—the fetal blood vessel that was her lifeline—it also kept her other blood vessels more open or dilated. And this was starting to cause problems with her stomach and intestines. She began vomiting her feedings and was increasingly irritable and fussy. She didn't even calm down when her mother held her, sometimes for hours. A decision needed to be made.

Stephanie was one of the most remarkable NICU social workers I've met in my career. From her, I learned the art of delivering bad news, how to deal with death and dying, and how to help parents cope with incredibly stressful situations. And Emily's family was a test case for all of those challenges. Stephanie arranged a family conference. It took some doing because of Emily's father's schedule and, I thought, his reluctance to deal with the situation. And who could blame him? He'd just embarked on a long, stressful residency training program, and he was clearly focused on that now and would need to be for several more years to come. How could he handle the terrible stress of raising a severely handicapped child with major medical problems? He'd also spent far less time with the baby than her mother had because of his work schedule. We all sensed that he was ready to say good-bye to her and not go forward with the surgery. Yet these were clearly *not* the same signals we were getting from her mother. She seemed to want, more than anything, to take Emily home and be a real mother for her, giving her whatever she needed. But did this also include every medical or surgical intervention?

During the conference, Emily's father began by asking more questions, trying to clarify what the choices were and what the future held. What exactly would be the sequence of events if she went for the first surgery? What could they expect if the prostaglandins were simply discontinued? Could they take her home? How long would she live? *How* would she live? What would she suffer, in either case? I found myself shaking inside. These were the very questions *I* would be asking if I were in his shoes, and yet I was the one giving the answers — to the best of my ability. Did my own feelings of what I would do influence what I told him? I still don't know. I suppose they did, but then, isn't that somehow expected? Perhaps even necessary?

Her mother just sat quietly, looking sad, but somehow calm and resigned, too. The Vietnamese interpreter helped to translate what I'd been saying to Emily's father, relieving him of the burden of trying to replay my answers to his agonizing questions to his wife.

In the end, we were all surprised when her father said, "We really appreciate all the information we've been given. As you can imagine, we've given this decision a lot of thought and now…we've decided to go ahead with the surgery. We think we have a pretty good idea of what the future holds, but my wife, in particular, is prepared to take what comes. She wants to give Emily the longest and best possible life and this seems to be the only way to do that." And then Emily's mother spoke, by way of the interpreter this time, instead of her husband. She said that in her country, parents took care of their children, no matter how serious their birth defects and no matter how disabled they were or would become. And that's what she was prepared to do with Emily. She knew that because her husband's career was on the line, most of Emily's care would fall to her. And she was prepared to accept it, for the sake of both her husband and her daughter. "I'm her mother; she's my beloved daughter," she said in Vietnamese. "What choice do I really have?" Tears rolled silently down her face and the room fell silent after the translator had finished. I thought, how on earth do people cope with such terrible choices? And what would I do if I were in his shoes? What about *her* shoes?

Emily needed to be transferred to the university hospital across town for the heart surgery and so we busied ourselves over the next day or so, getting her *and* her parents ready. As so often happens, the staff had gotten rather attached to Emily and her parents and it was hard to say good-bye. I had a few moments alone with her father before they left with Emily in the transport ambulance. He stood with his fingers around Emily's tiny hand and said quietly, "I remember that moment after she was born when I realized something wasn't right. It was before you'd even spoken to us. And my first thought was that I couldn't handle this and a residency, too.

And I could tell that you knew what she had. You had this *look*. But that interesting case turned out to be Emily and I'm her father and somehow, I'm handling it."

He sighed deeply and then told me, "I'm taking a leave of absence from my residency program. Who knows? Maybe that will turn out to be the best decision I ever made."

It was the most we'd spoken since the day Emily was born. I told him how sorry I was for everything and how much I hoped that things would work out for the best—whatever that was. It sounded so lame. And then they were off.

A few days later, we heard that Emily had come through her first surgery with flying colors and was off the prostaglandin drip. Two weeks later, her father called the unit to let everyone know that she was going home. He asked, could they stop by the unit? To show her off?

And a few hours later, there they were. Emily's father held her and her mother fussed with her little jacket and hat while we all ooh'd and ah'd. She still had a feeding tube in her nose so we guessed that she wasn't nippling all her feeds yet, but at least she was fairly pink and wasn't tethered to an IV for her prostaglandin drip. Who knew what life had in store for them all, but at least they would have a chance to be a family together, in their own home, and with their own hopes and expectations for their unique little girl. We all wished them well.

CHAPTER 9

Travis

O NE OF THE most interesting aspects of my neonatology fellowship training involved "going on transport." In the 1980s, San Francisco had a relatively low birth rate compared to other major cities, but the state of California had one of the highest birth rates in the country with many births occurring in rural areas, particularly during the busy harvest times, when no one could be spared in order to take a pregnant woman to a faraway city hospital for a high-risk delivery. So a system had been established years ago that involved hospitals in major cities sending out transport teams to bring the sickest babies from the "field" to their NICUs. I had done a fair number of transports in Cleveland when I was a pediatric resident, but those had all been within driving distance of the hospital, so we could go out by ambulance. We called it "riding the range."

In California, on the other hand, most of the transports were done by air. We'd get the call, assemble all our equipment—including the transport incubator—and we'd wheel it all into an ambulance that would take us to the airport. There, we'd board a small brown plane (excellent fodder for baby poop jokes) and off we'd go. Local ambulances would take us, with our equipment, from the plane to the hospital. Sometimes we'd land at one of the small coastal airstrips, go to the hospital, and get the baby ready for transport, and then the fog would come in and we'd be unable to take off. And then there were times when we'd have to wheel the heavy transport incubator from the ambulance to the hospital along dirt paths lining cow pastures — and get stuck in the mud on the way to the nursery. But the most interesting aspects of the job were the babies themselves. You just never knew what you were going to find once you got there.

We got the call about Travis on a gorgeous fall day. *At least it'll be a good day to fly*, I thought as Joe — one of our transport nurses — and I got things ready. Travis was born on his due date after a pretty uneventful pregnancy, but you couldn't say the same about his teenage mother's long, difficult labor and emergency cesarean section delivery. Travis was described by the local pediatrician as being "stunned" at birth. He didn't cry and he was covered in thick meconium — that first poop that babies sometimes had *in utero* due to the stress of the birth process. The doctor had "sucked him out" (nursery lingo for placing a tube in his windpipe and then applying suction to remove any meconium lodged there, preventing it from getting into his lungs). It then took a while to "get him going" — meaning getting him to cry, breathe, and turn that nice pink color babies should have by the time they're about five minutes old.

His Apgar scores were low — these are really the first "grades" that babies get — reflecting the difficulties he had with that miraculous transition from fetus to newborn. The pediatrician had brought him to the hospital's tiny special care nursery, where babies could receive additional care such as oxygen and IV medications. In this particular hospital, an old infant ventilator collected dust in a corner of a utility room.

The pediatrician had called us to transport Travis when he was only a few hours old. He was breathing faster than normal and was requiring about 50 percent oxygen in order to keep him pink (we normally breathe 21 percent oxygen). But he apparently didn't look pasty (which would indicate low blood pressure and skin perfusion) and the initial blood work they'd been able to obtain looked good—no significant acid in the blood and a normal white blood cell count. This made us think it was less likely that an infection was causing his breathing problems. They'd also been able to get an IV in one of his scalp veins and had started antibiotics, just in case. Overall he seemed stable, but clearly he was more than this small community hospital could handle. It was always better to transport babies while they were stable and get them to a higher-level NICU—just in case they got worse.

While Joe and I finished collecting our equipment and getting the transport incubator ready, one of the attending neonatologists—Barry—continued talking to the pediatrician, advising him regarding certain aspects of the baby's care. He hung up the phone just as we were heading out the door to the waiting ambulance that would take us to the airport. "This kid sounds pretty stable, Chris," he said, "just pack him up and see if you can get back before the sun goes down." In other words, it was hoped that Travis was going to be a classic "scoop and run."

It took Joe and me about two hours to get from hospital door to hospital door. The ride down the coast was beautiful, with minimal turbulence. Those small transport planes were *not* always a smooth ride; one of my colleagues always took a Dramamine before he went out on transport.

When we walked into the hospital's special care nursery, it was quiet—a little *too* quiet. As was typically the case at the smaller community hospitals, Travis was the only baby in there. He was lying on a warmer with a clear-walled square box (an oxygen "hood") over his head and he was breathing so fast, he couldn't cry even if he'd wanted to. The pediatrician who'd called us a few hours earlier had done what Barry had asked him to do and then gone back to his office, where he likely had dozens of patients impatiently waiting for him.

The lone hospital nurse in the room handed Joe the latest lab results and started filling him in on Travis's first few hours of life, addressing him respectfully as "Doctor." This was not unusual. If I went out on transport with a male nurse, or even if I walked into the room with a male ambulance driver, the hospital staff (which sometimes included the pediatrician) would assume *he* was the doctor and I was the nurse. Instead of joining them, I went over to where Travis lay spread-eagled on a warming table.

A woman who appeared to be about my age was standing by the table, staring at the baby. I introduced myself as the transport doctor from San Francisco and when I found out that she was Travis's grandmother, I realized that she herself must have been a teenager when she gave birth to Travis's mother. I explained what we were going to do and assured her that we would stop by her daughter's room on our way out, so that she could see and touch her baby before he flew off to San Francisco. Travis's grandmother became very agitated then. "Didn't they tell you? She's giving the baby up for adoption. No way should she see him. No way."

Now was not the time to get into an argument. And I had work to do with Travis. I told her we would get back to her on that, but right now I needed to see Travis and get him taken care of. I asked her to leave the nursery for 30 minutes or so. Reluctantly, she did so. I did a brief exam, noting first that Travis was a big, well-developed baby—nearly nine pounds. When I put a stethoscope to his chest, I heard very noisy breath sounds—probably due to inhaling some of that meconium before or during his birth, which was confirmed when I looked at his chest X-ray. He was also quite pale, and now he *was* pasty looking and in addition to breathing fast, his heart rate was higher than normal.

He looked sick and not at all as I'd expected, based on that initial phone call. I increased the oxygen level on his hood and turned to the staff nurse, who was still talking to Joe (even though by then, he'd clearly told her that *he* was the transport nurse and *I* was the transport doctor). I asked the staff nurse whether anyone had gotten a blood pressure reading and she said no. Did I want one done? If so, she'd have to leave the room and find a baby cuff and blood pressure machine. At "home," we took so many simple things for granted, such as getting a baby's blood pressure. I asked myself, would a blood pressure reading really change anything that I was about to do? The answer was no. On the other hand, it was one of those important numbers we liked for documentation on the transport record. And it would give the hospital's staff something to do. So I said yes, I really needed a blood pressure reading.

Joe assured her that he had the right size baby cuff, but we did need a blood pressure machine. She left to find one, and Joe and I went over to Travis's warming table together. I could tell that his reaction to the baby was the same as mine.

"Jeez," Joe said, "this kid looks sick. And just wait till you see the blood gas they got." I glanced at the blood gas lab result that he held out to me, and at first I couldn't believe it. It was very bad—low oxygen level, high carbon dioxide, and lots of acid.

Joe and I looked at each other and we said, nearly simultaneously, "He needs to be intubated." We needed to get control of Travis's airway and essentially take over his breathing while we tried to stabilize him for the transport. This was no small task in a community hospital. For one thing, we'd have to breathe for him by hand, not just at the hospital but the whole way back to San Francisco. Today, transport incubators come with wonderful little baby ventilators attached to them, but back in the early 1980s, about all they provided was warmth. I would have to manually inflate the baby's lungs.

What worried me the most was the procedure itself. I wasn't really concerned about getting the tube in—I'd successfully intubated at least 100 babies by that time—but I was nervous about what the procedure would do to Travis. I'd seen babies who were barely hanging on completely fall apart after they were intubated. And I had an awful feeling that Travis could be one of those babies.

"Joe, check our drug box and see what we've got."

I was thinking that we'd need some morphine to sedate him before putting the tube in, and then a slew of drugs to get him stable enough for the transport. That would include dopamine or other "pressors" to bring up his blood pressure (which I assumed was already too low), bicarbonate to treat his high acid level, calcium to strengthen his failing heart, and various emergency medications like adrenaline or epinephrine in case things got really bad and we had to "Code" him.

Joe took out the intubation equipment and looked through the rest of the box to see what we had brought with us. It didn't look good. Nobody thought Travis would be this sick and so Joe had packed only one vial of each drug, including the emergency medications. He found the morphine, gave Travis a dose through his tiny scalp IV, and we got ready for the intubation. The hospital nurse had not yet returned with the blood pressure machine, so we decided to go ahead without her. And Travis did not like the procedure one little bit.

I got the tube in on the first try, but Travis's heart rate, which had been too high at 180 beats per minute, was suddenly dangerously low—50, by the end of the procedure. His monitor alarm was going off and he looked even more dreadful. What had we done? When she heard the commotion, the staff nurse came running in, pushing an adult blood pressure machine in front of her.

"Forget about the blood pressure!" I yelled. "We need some help here."

"But he was doing just fine before you came in!" she cried. "Are you sure you know what you're doing? Why is he intubated? Do you want me to call the doctor?"

That was all I needed. Inside, I was in turmoil. I really *wasn't* sure what I was doing. But I did trust my gut instincts, and these were screaming that this kid was very sick and was going to need everything I could think of to keep him alive for the transport to San Francisco. Having a baby die at the referring hospital or, worse, die on the way back was everyone's worst transport nightmare.

While I "bagged" the baby—breathing for him by hand with a rubber bag attached to an oxygen hose—Joe drew up all the emergency drugs we had in our box. I began ordering them, one by one, until I started seeing some gradual improvement in his heart rate and color. And then I ordered a dopamine drip, which Joe began to prepare, using the one vial of dopamine that we had. I knew that Travis's blood pressure was probably so low that it wouldn't have registered on the standard baby machine—if the nurse had been able to find one. Dopamine would help to get the blood pressure up.

I kept on bagging the baby while Joe set up the intravenous infusion he'd prepared. It was then that he noticed that the tiny scalp IV the pediatrician had inserted a few hours earlier was a "goner." It had infiltrated, filling the skin around it with fluid because it had slipped out of the vein. Or worse—perhaps it had never been in. Joe and I looked at each other. It was possible that the baby had never gotten any of the medications we'd given, or perhaps any of the medications *they'd* given. The latter included the antibiotics. And this baby was acting septic—as though he had a bloodstream infection that had started in the womb, planting its deadly seeds in a very vulnerable soil. What if he hadn't gotten the antibiotics that we assumed had been given in the first few hours of life? I decided to assume the worst. The downside of giving an extra dose would clearly be offset by giving the antibiotics now if they'd never been

given initially. And another thing—this baby needed more secure
vascular access if we were going to get him to San Francisco. I
would need to put in an umbilical vessel catheter.

Umbilical catheter insertion could take up to an hour in the
nice, controlled setting of a NICU. You usually needed to prepare
the cord with an antiseptic, place sterile towels around the site, and
don a sterile gown, cap, and gloves. And sometimes it was hard
to advance the catheter once you got it through the opening that
you'd carefully dilated. I needed access and I needed it now, so I
cut corners and proceeded to do the fastest umbilical artery and
vein catheter placement I'd ever done. I did have the presence of
mind to draw a blood culture before I had Joe administer the extra
antibiotic doses. We later heard that that blood culture was positive for *Escherichia coli*, a nasty gram-negative organism that causes
septic shock.

Travis had achieved a marginal level of stability—at least he
had a relatively normal heart rate and reasonable color. My own
heart was racing, though, from the adrenaline surge that a crisis
always brings on, and my hand was starting to get fatigued from
bagging him. But there was no way we could attach his tube to the
hospital's dusty old ventilator, even if we could figure out how to
use it. I'd learned that babies like Travis became very touchy with
any changes, and that included having someone else, or a machine,
take over their breathing. I'd gotten a good feel for Travis's lung
compliance and his touchiness. I knew that either Joe or I was
going to have to breathe for him for the next few hours, until we
got him back to the unit.

I needed to call "home" and ask for advice from Barry, the
attending neonatologist. I looked at my watch and realized we'd
been gone four hours! By now, everyone back in the unit had to
be wondering what had happened to us. But someone would have
to take over bagging Travis while I was on the phone. There was

a respiratory therapist at the hospital who'd arrived in the room a few minutes earlier, and he volunteered to take over. Joe and I hesitated, but we had so much to do and this guy said he'd bagged babies before and he looked competent. I showed him what I'd been doing, which seemed to be working, and he took over. It came as no surprise that Travis didn't like the change at first. His heart rate started to drop and his color changed from pinkish to blue. But gradually he started to respond to the new hands, and I felt as though this was my only chance to get some much-needed advice.

Joe had already gotten Barry on the phone for me and had started filling him in. So when I got on the line, I just said, "Barry, this kid is really, really sick. I don't know if we're going to get him back alive." He asked me a couple of questions and then said, "Chris, I don't have any magic advice. Just give him lots of morphine to keep him calm and don't be afraid to keep giving him epi if his heart rate keeps dropping. And get the hell out of there." It was good just to hear his voice and to know that everyone was going to be ready to take over once we got back. I asked a couple of more specific questions, then hung up the phone and returned to Travis's bedside. The respiratory therapist was relieved to give the bag back to me; his hand was already getting tired. How was I going to do this all the way back to San Francisco?

Before Joe started getting Travis ready to move to our transport incubator, he took another look at our transport drug box. I heard a sharp intake of breath from him—we'd already used up most of the drugs we'd brought with us. And replacement vials wouldn't be easy to come by at this local hospital. The drugs we'd brought with us had been specially prepared in dilutions that were designed for the tiny doses babies received. We were going to have to get by with what we had. And we really needed to get going. Travis was not going to like being moved from the warmer to the transport incubator.

I briefly contemplated sending word to the postpartum ward where Travis's mother was recovering from her C-section, asking them to bring her to us. This could save us some precious time. But I remembered what I'd promised his grandmother, and I knew that there was a possibility that this was going to be the first and last time Travis's mother would see him alive. We had to stop by her room and give her some time to be with him and to kiss him good-bye, maybe forever.

While the hospital nurse stood by, watching us suspiciously, Joe and I readied the transport incubator and started moving everything that we could into it—saving Travis for last. Finally we were ready. We gave the baby a good dose of morphine, and then I disconnected the bag and Joe picked him up and quickly placed him in the incubator. We hooked everything back up and held our breath. Time elapsed: 90 seconds. And Travis crashed. His heart rate had dropped as soon as I stopped bagging him, and now it plummeted. I bagged him desperately, giving him over 100 breaths per minute, but I just couldn't get him back. I felt panicky.

"Another dose of epi!" I shouted to Joe, who had already drawn up drugs into syringes in preparation for this. But this time it didn't help at all. What the hell was happening? And then it hit me. That new pair of hands had been bagging his fragile lungs with who knew how much pressure. He must have "blown a pneumo." Part of his lung must have ruptured, spilling air into the pleural cavity around it. This would gradually cause his lung to collapse. For a touchy baby like Travis, a pneumothorax was the kiss of death.

"Get me a couple of 23-gauge butterfly needles!" I shouted to the hospital nurse, who was looking terrified. Luckily, she knew where to find these and brought over a whole box. Meanwhile, Joe had started cardiopulmonary resuscitation because Travis's heart rate was so low. This meant that there were now four adult hands in that small transport incubator, and there were soon going to be six—someone was going to have to bag Travis while I tried to evacuate the pleural air. And if I got lots of air out of Travis's chest with the needles, I'd need to put in a chest tube in order to keep evacuating air on the way back. The respiratory therapist took over the bagging again; Joe briefly stopped doing CPR so I could put the first needle in, on top of the right side of Travis's chest. I felt it "pop," and then I started drawing out air with a large syringe. Lots of air. It just kept coming, and as it did, Travis started to come back. His heart rate, which had dropped to zero, reappeared on the monitor screen. First 20, then 30, 40, 50, and finally 60. This was still way too low, but at least he was alive.

I knew there had to be air on the other side, too. I handed the syringe attached to the first needle to Joe, who continued drawing out air. Then I did the same procedure on the left side of his chest. And got the same result—lots of air. Now Travis really responded. His heart rate climbed back up to normal, although his color still looked dreadful. Bilateral pneumothoraces, in a very sick baby. I would now need to place two chest tubes. This was truly a transport from hell.

There was absolutely no way that I could put in chest tubes while Travis was in the transport incubator, so now we had to move him back to the hospital warming table. Luckily, he tolerated this much better than he had the first time—probably because he didn't have all that extra air in his chest. We gave him more morphine—chest tubes were painful—and a paralyzing drug. I didn't want him to fight the ventilator bag I was squeezing and rupture more of his lungs. I'd put in lots of chest tubes when I was a resident, so fortunately the procedure went smoothly.

Joe had brought the terrified hospital nurse over and showed her how to keep sucking air out of Travis's chest with the syringes attached to both needles. Having an important job to do in the midst of a major crisis brought about a complete change in her attitude toward us. She was now part of the team, and the team was, at least temporarily, winning the game.

I sewed the two chest tubes in place and Joe expertly placed a dressing over each, using lots of tape to help keep them secure. Each tube was attached to a Heimlich valve, which we could use to keep any extra air flowing out of the chest while we forced air in with the bag. Now we were ready, once again, to move Travis to the transport incubator. This time it went more smoothly. He still didn't like it, but at least we didn't have to resuscitate him. He was now quite heavily sedated, with all the morphine we'd given him, and I hoped the effects would last for the trip back.

I was exhausted. Worse, I needed to go to the bathroom. But I'd taken over the bagging over from the respiratory therapist and I'd gotten into a nice rhythm that Travis seemed to like. It was time to move. I'd just have to hold it—something I'd gotten used to doing as a resident—and I turned down someone's offer of a Coke. Joe called the airport to let the pilot know we'd be ready to take off within the hour. And the hospital nurse called for the ambulance driver to come take us back to the airport. I realized that I didn't even know her name. "It's Shelly," she said, "and you were really amazing. I hope he makes it, after all that."

"Me too," I said, "and thanks for all your help. It's really hard to just jump right in there and do what you need to do, but you did—and we really needed your help." At that, she just beamed.

We'd now been at this hospital for three hours, but before we could get into the ambulance and start the two-hour trip back to San Francisco we needed to wheel the incubator, with all our stuff piled on top of it, to Travis's mother's room. Even though his grandmother seemed adamantly opposed to it, I knew that this might be the first and last chance his mother would have to see him alive. And I needed to tell her something about what was happening to him.

Placing both my hands through the porthole doors of the transport incubator, I continued bagging Travis as we moved slowly down the hospital corridor. I kept a watchful eye on his color and the heart rate monitor on the side of the incubator. So far, so good.

We rolled into Room 22 and there, on the hospital bed, lay a giggling, tattooed, very large, very young woman. And lying next to her on the bed was a scruffy, dirty, similarly tattooed young man—boy, really—with his mouth on her breast. Joe and I exchanged glances—what a family scene to walk in on! But we had a mission. Travis's mother (and possibly, his father) needed to see him and touch him, and hear just a bit about him before we left the hospital. The baby's grandmother, whom I'd spoken with hours earlier, snored quietly in a rocking chair next to the bed.

"Sandy Watkins?" I asked. (It was always good to confirm that you were in the right room.)

"Yeah, that's me," she said, as her boyfriend slowly disengaged himself from her and sat up in the bed. "Is that my baby?" she asked.

"Yes, that's him," I said, "and I heard that you named him Travis."

"That's *his* name," she said, pointing to her boyfriend. I guessed that meant that he was Travis's father.

"Well, I'm Dr. Gleason, and this is Joe Janus. We're taking Travis to San Francisco to our Neonatal Intensive Care Unit. He's really sick and needs to be on a respirator. That's what I'm doing right now with this bag. It's attached to a breathing tube going to his lungs on one end and that oxygen tank on the other end."

She said, "Well, what's wrong with him?"

By this time, her mother had woken up in the chair next to the bed and was listening, too. Her boyfriend, on the other hand, was already nodding off as I was speaking. I explained that Travis was very, very sick. He could have gotten an infection in the womb, but we wouldn't know that for a couple of days—just like with a strep throat culture. I told them we were doing everything we could to get him to San Francisco and to save his life, but that we might lose him on the way.

"You mean, he could *die*?" his mother said. Now, I knew that at least some of what I'd said had sunk in.

"Yes, he could die," I said. "He nearly died already, when both his lungs popped about an hour ago."

At this, her boyfriend opened his eyes and leaned over her to see what I was talking about. The two of them peered through the Plexiglas walls into the incubator. Their baby wasn't moving at all because of the drugs we'd given him. He just lay there, with his chest going up and down with each breath that I gave him with the bag.

"Can I touch him?" his mother whispered.

"Of course you can," I said—but this was easier said than done. I had one of my hands in each of the two portholes. I decided to disconnect the bag from the tube briefly so I could open the entire door and let her have a good look at her son. Joe helped me move the incubator right next to her bed and I actually climbed on the bed, asking her boyfriend to scoot up a bit. Now they could both reach in and touch Travis while I continued to bag him. His mother took one of his fingers into her hand and started stroking it, and her boyfriend patted his head. No one said a word. No tears were shed. But Travis's mother, a child herself, seemed to grow up in front of my eyes.

And then I realized that Travis's heart rate was slowing down. Air was probably accumulating in his chest again; we needed to actively pull it off from those two chest tubes. Joe had grabbed the Polaroid camera when we'd left our unit, and he quickly snapped a picture, getting as close as he could to Travis's face. Then I jumped off the bed and we moved around the incubator, and Joe started sucking air out with the syringes we'd tossed into the incubator. Thankfully, Travis responded. But we knew that time was of the essence—we had to get out of there.

"We really have to get going now; we'll take good care of him and I'll call you the minute we get there," I said, as calmly as I could. Inwardly, though, I was a wreck. How was I going to keep him going for the next two hours? And how was I going to keep myself going? I still had to pee and I needed caffeine or sugar, something. Joe handed them the picture he'd taken and we left them all there, staring silently at it.

Joe and I moved into the hall, with me still bagging Travis, Joe making sure all our stuff stayed either in or on top of the incubator, and the ambulance driver pushing the heavy wheeled incubator along. I saw a restroom sign, and knew it was now or never. I gave the bag to Joe and made a run for it. It was a relief in more ways than one, including just having a moment to myself away from such a dire situation.

On the way out of the hospital, we passed a soda machine and the ambulance driver got Joe and me each a Coke. I didn't think I'd actually be able to drink it unless we could find a straw, but it was nice knowing that it was there.

The next two hours seemed like ten. The back of the transport plane was cramped and incredibly noisy. Joe and I could barely hear each other, so we used a lot of finger pointing and mouthing of words. The incubator was secured to a heavy metal bar on one side and we sat on two small jump seats on the other side, directly opposite the incubator portholes. If I craned my neck, I could stick my head through the cockpit door and shout to the pilot. We had seatbelts with shoulder harnesses, but I couldn't quite reach Travis with mine on, so I hoped there wouldn't be a lot of turbulence. I never really thought about a plane crash. The tackle box, with all our drugs and equipment, lay unsecured and open, right next to Joe.

Travis's lungs got stiffer and stiffer as we flew along the Pacific coast. I needed to bag harder and harder just to move his chest, and my hand started to get very sore. His heart rate kept dropping and we kept pulling extra air from his chest. Toward the end, that didn't help anymore so we started pushing the epi. The pilot asked if we wanted to have emergency clearance for landing, and Joe and I looked at each other briefly and then simultaneously shouted yes.

By the time we landed at SFO, we'd used up all the drugs we'd brought along. Normally I'm not thrilled with ambulance drivers using lights and sirens on transports, but this time I wasn't worried about an accident. I just wanted to get there…to get home and hand this terrible case over to someone else. So we "red-lighted" it all the way, even going the wrong way on a one-way street to avoid a traffic jam.

The pilot had called the hospital NICU when we'd landed (no cell phones in those days) and gave them our estimated time of arrival. When we screeched into the parking lot behind the hospital, there they were, ready and waiting for us. I was never so glad to see a group of people in my life. And Travis was still alive—barely, but he actually had a heart rate and a bit of color to his lips. I continued to bag him, because now was not the time for a transition to another pair of hands.

Five minutes later, we walked into the unit. I felt as if I were coming home to my family after a long and harrowing adventure. After demonstrating what I'd been doing with the bag, I handed it over to one of our respiratory therapists who, as everyone agreed, could "bag a rock." And several nurses began moving all the equipment over to the warming table to which we would transfer Travis. The chest tubes would be hooked up to suction machines that would continuously pull out the extra air. And there were drugs lined up in little bags at the end of the bed, ready for use. It was all so reassuring, so high tech, so familiar.

Once Travis was moved over to his warming bed and was relatively stable, Joe and I gave our brief report to the NICU team—the attending, fellow, resident, and admitting nurse. I summarized what I'd gleaned from the medical record and Joe recounted the hospital nurse's story (which I'd missed because she assumed Joe was the doctor). I briefly outlined what had happened, hoping against hope that I'd done the right thing and hadn't missed something obvious that could have prevented the baby's downhill spiral. But actually, I think everyone in that room was just amazed that Travis was not dead on arrival. And so were we. We then answered a few pointed questions from the assembled group: When did you give the antibiotics? Did you get a blood culture? Where's the last chest X-ray? What drugs did you give him? Both Joe and I would fill in detailed transport records afterward, but the team needed certain information *now*.

I wasn't too surprised that no one asked about the parents, although we prided ourselves on being very family centered, a novel concept in those days. Travis needed so much immediate attention that no one had much time to think about the family. But I did say that they were teenagers, that I'd shown them the baby, and that Joe had taken a snapshot. This also would be in my written transport note, but I knew that everyone there would want to know *something* about this baby's family—because by this time, almost everyone there expected him to die.

After we were finished with our report, Joe and I sat down to fill out our transport records (separate ones for the doctor and the nurse), and I finally could have my Coke. There have been a few food or drink "moments" in my life that I can vividly recall, and that was one of them. That Coke was so delicious that I actually remember licking my lips after each long sip. I still love Coke, although now I usually drink Caffeine-Free Diet Coke, which is nowhere near as delicious.

Before I left the unit I remembered that I'd promised to call Travis's mother, so I pulled out the scrap of paper in my pocket with the hospital switchboard and her room number on it and called from the phone nearest to where Travis was being worked on. He'd had another dive in his heart rate and color, and he was getting another chest tube put in—his third—as I dialed the number. The situation didn't look good, but at least he'd made it to our unit. The hospital operator was ringing the room, but no one was answering. Where could they be? I wondered. Finally, after at least a dozen rings, a sleepy man's voice answered the phone. Must be the boyfriend, I thought, as he mumbled something about Travis's mother being in the bathroom—for a very long time, it appeared. I told him the good news first. Travis had made it to San Francisco and was now in the unit, and everything possible was being done to save his life. He didn't say anything, and then I told him the bad news: that Travis was still critically ill and that I wasn't sure he was going to make it. There still was no response, so I asked if he had any questions. There was a pause, and then he said, "Travis is not my son. That was two boyfriends ago. You better talk to Sandy." So I waited for a few minutes until the baby's mother came back to her bed.

When she got on the phone, I told her the same things I'd told her boyfriend, ending with how critically ill Travis was—in fact, he was being resuscitated right next to me as we spoke. She didn't say anything at first, but when I asked her if she had any questions, she paused and then asked me when he could be circumcised. His father (who was not the boy I'd met, she whispered) was circumcised, and so Travis should be, too. She really wanted to know when it could be done. I did spend a few minutes talking about circumcision with her, but then I tried to come back to the reality of the situation. And she just kept coming back to that circumcision. It hit me, finally, that this was the only way she could cope with this impending tragedy—to focus on the one thing she'd thought about before she'd delivered Travis: the foreskin of his penis.

Later that night, after I'd gone home, showered, and had my favorite sandwich—liverwurst and honey—I called the unit to find out how things were going. Travis was still being hand bagged, but he finally had a stable blood pressure and he hadn't been Coded for the past two hours. As I hung up the phone and prepared to hit the sack, bits and pieces of that transport from hell kept coming back to me. Did I pick up that pneumothorax too late? Did *I* give him a pneumothorax because I didn't bag him right? Did he "crump," or get worse, because of something I'd done? Should I have started the dopamine sooner? Could I have missed something, such as a heart defect? These were all essentially the same question we all asked ourselves at one time or another when we faced difficult clinical situations and bad things happened: *Did I screw up?*

Amazingly, Travis lived. He went home three weeks later with his teenage mother, although we all assumed he would actually be raised by his grandmother. And he went home without his foreskin.

CHAPTER 10

Joshua

WE WERE LUCKY enough to get a table by the window at the rooftop bar of the Mark Hopkins Hotel. I would be coming on service in the NICU at Mt. Zion Hospital the next morning and I needed to hear the important details about the babies currently in the unit from the fellow, Dave, who was going off service. Over the past year, we'd gotten into the habit of doing this hand-off proce-dure over a couple of drinks at selected rooftop bars in major San Francisco hotels. Tonight it was the Mark Hopkins.

After we'd ordered our Manhattans and a plateful of hors d'oeuvres, Dave quietly began to go through the list he'd prepared for me. There were 20 patients on the ICU team; the other 10 patients in the NICU were on the noncritical, intermediate care team. We called most of the babies on the latter team "gainers and growers"—premature babies who were over the critical phase of their early entry into the world and now just needed to basically get bigger. As neonatal fellows, we weren't assigned to that team because there was just too much for us to learn about the critically ill babies. And the truth is, we all thought that the "gainer and growers" could be, well…boring.

The babies on Dave's list—soon to be mine—were definitely not boring. Most were classified as critical, although some were more critical than others. Dave went through those babies first. During our inaugural hand-off session at a rooftop bar, we'd both realized that we needed to complete our work *before* we had our drinks, and it was also a good idea to have the key points in writing to refer to the next day on rounds. So Dave had prepared a team list, and next to each baby's name he'd neatly written the bare essentials about that child. This list also allowed us to avoid mentioning any patient by name, which would have been a terrible invasion of privacy if anyone else were to overhear our conversation, however quietly we tried to speak.

We always started with the sickest patient and today this was Baby Lockwood, a premature baby boy who'd seemed to have absolutely everything go wrong that could go wrong. We spent several minutes talking about his laundry list of problems—chronic lung disease, sepsis, bowel perforation, head bleed, brittle bones—and his parents. How were they coping with all this? What could we do to help *them* while we worked to pull their baby through?

Once he'd finished discussing the toughest patient, Dave proceeded down his list, going much faster as he went along. Just as we were taking the first sip of our drinks, he got to the last patient on the list. He pointed to the name—Berk—as he gave me the nitty gritty about him: "This is a seven-week-old former 28-week preemie who was really sick for the first couple days of his life. But then amazingly, he just turned around and came off the ventilator. He never had a head bleed and never developed chronic lung disease. And he was on full tube feedings by the time he was one month old. No more IVs."

This was pretty unusual. Premature baby boys, on average, had a rougher NICU course than premature baby girls. They usually had worse lung disease and were generally more immature, taking longer to tolerate their feedings and to remember to breathe. And white boys, on average, were the worst. "Wimpy white males" we'd call them. I knew that this baby must have been doing extremely well if he'd gotten all the way to full feedings, without chronic lung disease and without a bad head bleed, by the time he was a month old.

"Of course, he's still having As and Bs, so he's not ready to go home yet," Dave said, meaning that he needed to be monitored because he occasionally forgot to breathe (apnea) and when that happened, his heart rate slowed down (bradycardia).

"So, what's he doing on our team?" I asked. "How come he's not a 'gainer and grower'?"

"He's got hernias now, on both sides, and they're really getting big—soon they'll be down to his knees."

We both laughed. Preemie boys, especially the ones born the earliest in gestation, often developed inguinal hernias because their testicles hadn't completely descended. This left a nice opening—the "inguinal ring"—from the scrotum to the abdominal cavity through which a loop (or two) of intestine could poke, or herniate. Baby boys eventually needed to have their hernias repaired surgically, but we'd usually postpone it until they were fully recovered and more mature, especially if they'd been very sick initially and still had significant lung disease. But if the hernias were huge, as they apparently were in this little guy, we'd often schedule them for surgery a week or so before they went home so the parents wouldn't have to worry about the baby getting an incarceration, which occurred when the intestine could not be "reduced" from the scrotum back into the abdomen. Under such circumstances, it could swell and eventually become gangrenous.

"Oh, and I can't believe I nearly forgot to tell you this," Dave said, lowering his voice to a whisper, even though there was no one close to our table. "There are major social issues. The baby's parents are Orthodox Jews and run a small Hebrew school in Los Angeles. They were visiting friends up here when she suddenly went into labor and they couldn't stop it. She wound up having a C-section because the baby was breech. And get this: the dad had to fly back three days after the baby was born because school was opening for their fall session. At least the baby was more or less out of the woods by then."

"That must have been really hard, for both of them," I said.

"Well, that's not the worst of it," Dave went on. "While the OBs were in there doing the C-section, they discovered that her belly was full of fluid, and tumor cells, as it turned out. She's been diagnosed with advanced ovarian cancer."

"Oh my God!" I exclaimed. "How on earth could anyone deal with all that at once? Your first baby is a preemie and then you find out you've got cancer?"

We were both silent for a few minutes, quietly sipping our drinks and gazing out at the beautiful San Francisco skyline. Dave and I had become very good friends during our fellowship, sharing a lot of our self-doubt and angst with each other. We'd learned a lot about each other during the process. I knew we were both thinking the same thing but couldn't find words to express it. It could just as easily have been us, and what would *we* have done?

The next morning, I took the early 38 Geary bus from my apartment near Point Lobos to the hospital. Although I still had my grandmother's 1971 orange Dodge Dart Swinger, I rarely drove it to the hospital because it was so difficult to find parking and if I was busy all day or up all night on call, I didn't quite trust myself to drive home safely. As I settled into my seat on the bus, I took out Dave's sign-out list and read over my notes, trying to get myself prepared for morning rounds and the day ahead. When I got to the end of the list and read over the notes I'd made on the Berk baby, I sat back for a moment and thought about the baby's mother.

I assumed that Stephanie, the unit's social worker, was helping in any way she could to make the situation somehow bearable. But really, what could anyone do? And how could I talk with this baby's mother about such relatively mundane preemie matters like As and Bs or hernia repairs, knowing that she would very likely not live to celebrate her son's first birthday?

I got off the bus and walked the short distance to the hospital, taking the elevator to the fifth floor of the pavilion where the NICU was located. When I opened the swinging door onto the unit I saw chaos, and my heart briefly sank. Coming on service was hard anyway—similar in a way to the first day on a new job—but when the unit was busy and everyone was running around, it was much harder. John, the fellow who'd been on the night before, was hand-bagging a big full-term baby. He looked exhausted, and when I walked over to the bedside and quietly reached for the bag, he gratefully gave it up to me. That baby was the only admission he'd gotten that night and the rest of the NICU was pretty quiet—even the sick Lockwood baby had actually been relatively stable. But, as we often reminded each other, it takes only one very sick baby to destroy your night.

John quickly gave me the baby's brief life history and the main events of the night. This was one of those babies who just had not made the normal circulatory transition from fetus to newborn. Her lung blood vessels were very touchy—clamping down at the slightest provocation, thereby limiting the amount of oxygen going to her body. She turned blue when she cried, when her diaper was changed, and finally, when she had to be intubated and placed on a ventilator. We called the condition PFC, persistent fetal circulation. Until the baby's lung circulation "cooled off" and those blood vessels stayed open, the way they were supposed to, we kept those babies very quiet, sedating and sometimes paralyzing them with drugs, trying not to do much to disturb them. I could see that one of the nurses had fashioned tiny ear muffs out of cotton balls for her, trying to decrease the stimulation that was bombarding her from all the noise and bustle of the NICU.

We all took turns hand-bagging that baby for the rest of the day and well into the night—me, the attending, and various respiratory therapists. Every time we tried to put her back on the ventilator she would "crump" and turn blue, and then it would take us awhile to get her pink again. Morning rounds were fragmented, not our typical well-organized bedside-to-bedside review with the residents and the attending physician. And I didn't have as much time as I would have liked to examine all those patients on Dave's list and to meet the parents who were there. I briefly examined the Berk baby, noting his hernias, which were indeed huge, but I didn't meet his mother. The nurses told me that she was between chemotherapy treatments and had decided to return to their school in Los Angeles for a few days. She had said she needed to do a few things before the baby's surgery. He had been scheduled for his hernia repair in a couple of days—along with a circumcision—and so I assumed I'd be meeting her soon. I hoped to have some time to talk to the unit's social worker, Stephanie, before she returned.

It was a very long night, but as dawn began to break we were finally able to stop hand-bagging that unstable baby girl. She had stayed on the ventilator for a full 30 minutes without turning blue and setting off any alarms. It looked as though she might actually be turning the corner. I hadn't slept all night and I badly needed a strong cup of coffee and a doughnut before morning rounds. It was 6:00 A.M., and that's when the little coffee shop downstairs opened. They had the best flavored coffees and fresh doughnuts. When I was on call "in house," I actually loved that early morning time, when the darkness of the night turned into day and the relief troops would begin to arrive. As I headed for the bank of elevators, one of them opened, and a rather gaunt, pale woman stepped out. She looked like she was wearing a wig, although I couldn't be sure. She was carrying a pink bakery box. We exchanged curious glances and then went our separate ways, I to get my coffee and doughnut and she, as it turned out, to visit her baby in the NICU.

When I returned to the NICU, I went straight to the staff lounge, a classroom-sized room just off the unit where all the staff—nurses, doctors, and respiratory therapists—gathered for their breaks, patient charting activities, and general schmoozing. A couple of the night nurses were clustered around a pink bakery box similar to the one I'd just seen carried by the woman coming off the elevator.

"Look at these things!" exclaimed Trisha, one of the night nurses. "They're so rich, you might as well just stick 'em right on your thigh."

"Berk's mom just brought them in," said Joe, one of the respiratory therapists. "She said she picked them up at a kosher bakery in L.A.—someplace near that school she and her husband run. Can you believe she could think about something like this, with everything else she must have on her mind?"

After I had peered into the box—but decided not to try one of the strange little pastries—I sank into one of the two overstuffed chairs in the corner of the room and began sipping my delicious hazelnut coffee and savoring each bite of my doughnut. I loved to watch the hustle and bustle of the change of shift going on in the room. Nearly everyone who came in the room peered into Mrs. Berk's pastry box. Few took anything from it.

Trisha decided to try one and sank into the other chair next to me with her pastry and a cup of coffee from the lounge's pot. We chatted for a bit about the night's events and then Trisha said, "Berk's mom's cancer is apparently so far advanced that there's nothing more they can do for her. I guess she's decided to enjoy whatever time she has left. It's just so hard to know what to say to her. I keep focusing on the baby, who's really doing well, and yet I really want to know how *she's* doing."

"I've been worrying about that since I got sign-out from Dave," I told her. "In a way, it was a relief not to have to think about it while I was concentrating on that new sick baby. Today, though, I'll have to deal with it. And I hope that Stephanie can help me do that."

I realized that our conversation was more about the two of us, and how we would deal with this terrible situation, than it was about the Berk baby or his cancer-stricken mom.

Morning rounds went much more smoothly than they had the day before. Everyone was thrilled at how well the new baby was doing—she'd stayed on the ventilator for several hours now without needing any hand-bagging—and I received kudos from the attending, which gave me a wonderful warm glow inside. Of course, I knew that in fact, I had little to do with her turnaround; if those blood vessels opened up, the babies did well no matter what you did, and if the vessels stayed closed, they died.

We ended rounds at Baby Berk's bedside. Jeff, the pediatric intern, briefly presented the baby's major issues: he was still having a few As and Bs, but none of them severe; he was nippling about half of his feeds (he received the rest via his gavage feeding tube); he was weaning from an incubator to a regular baby crib; and then there were those hernias. Jeff undid his diaper, which had barely contained them. His scrotum just sprang out as soon as the diaper was released. When Jeff pushed on one side of the scrotum, coaxing the herniated intestinal loops back up through the inguinal ring and thus demonstrating that his hernias were still reducible, the baby started to cry. And when he did, the increased pressure in his abdomen pushed those hernias literally down to his knees. I could see what Dave meant; these were hernias that really needed fixing. Before the baby went home, not after.

"So when is the hernia repair scheduled?" asked Susan, the attending physician.

"First thing Friday morning," answered Jeff. Today was Wednesday. "He's also scheduled for a circumcision and so for his Orthodox Jewish parents, it's also a religious ceremony, a bris. The family has found a local mohel who has surgical privileges at the hospital who can actually participate in the operation. Oh, and that's when the baby will get his name."

I had been wondering why he was still known as Baby Berk. Although we usually called babies by their last name, most of them actually did have a given name. It usually appeared on a cute little pink or blue card taped to the incubator, or sometimes written on a sibling's crayon drawing. But there wasn't anything like that at Baby Berk's bedside. I had been raised as an Episcopalian, but I'd attended a largely Jewish middle and high school and so was quite familiar with Jewish holidays like Rosh Hoshana and Yom Kippur and had attended my share of bar/bat mitzvahs, but I didn't know much about the bris ceremony. However, once, when I was a resident, I had watched a mohel perform a "circ" on a recovering preemie in the NICU, and I was impressed by how swiftly and seemingly painlessly he performed the surgical procedure.

After a brief team discussion of the baby's remaining medical issues, Jeff brought up the heavy social issues that were weighing on every member of the team. By then, we all knew that his mom had returned from her trip back home and had brought with her that box of kosher pastries for the staff. But in those days, parents were always asked to leave the unit while we did rounds, so she wasn't at the bedside when we started talking about her and her terrible situation. Stephanie, our social worker, joined us and began filling us in.

"I talked to her briefly this morning," she said. "She's losing the battle with her ovarian cancer, and she knows it. There really wasn't much hope to begin with. The disease was just too far advanced when it was discovered. So, she's decided to stop all the chemo and won't be doing any radiation. She wants to live well before she dies." We all stood there, lost in our own thoughts. And we probably would have stood there for a while longer if it hadn't been for Stephanie. She told us that if we wanted to talk with the baby's mom, we would have to wait until later in the afternoon when she would be back—from shopping at Loehmann's.

"They're having a sale," explained Stephanie. "It's a discount store, and they're having a sale. This is a dream come true for any hard-core shopper. She's going out there to do what she has to do—buy things for the baby, for her home, and for the school. She couldn't wait to get out there. I can't remember seeing anyone look quite so excited."

How could she have any interest in *shopping*? At first, I couldn't imagine myself doing something so ordinary, so mundane, if I were dying of cancer. I imagined traveling to some exotic place I'd always wanted to visit, or maybe trying some sort of adventure like skydiving. But *shopping*? I just didn't get it. And then it hit me. Stephanie had said she wanted to live well before she died. Shopping at Loehmann's *was* clearly an important part of her life, and she reveled in it—especially when they had a sale. Suddenly, I didn't feel any more anxiety about how I'd talk to her about her baby. She'd relish all those ordinary—yes, even boring—details about her son, too.

Rounds were over, and I had a couple of hours to examine the sickest patients and prepare a brief sign-out sheet for the fellow who would be on call that night. I didn't get interrupted with a delivery, and the unit was much more stable than it had been the day before, which was a good thing. After being up for 36 hours, I would invariably start to fade. Strange words would start coming out of my mouth when I was in the middle of a conversation and I would suddenly realize that I was daydreaming out loud. It was almost like having an "out of body" experience, and I was glad I didn't need to do anything very important. Later, when I became an attending physician, I would worry more about my state of mind after a long sleepless night in the NICU. Then, despite my fatigue, I would remain in charge, and I *would* need to make tough decisions and lead the team through any continuing crises. But for now, I was a fellow and I could go home, put it all out of my mind, and get some rest before starting again the next day.

As I sank into my seat on the 38 Geary bus, heading home, I reflected briefly on the past 36 hours. At least no one had died on my watch, and that sick baby girl had turned around. I wondered what the day had been like for the Berk baby's mother. Had she actually been able to enjoy her shopping trip?

When I got home, all I could manage for dinner was a bowl of split pea soup, which I ate while watching a rerun of *M*A*S*H*, my favorite TV show. I was in bed by 7:30 and slept like a rock until the alarm went off at 6:30 the next morning. It was Thursday, and I was hoping that the sick baby girl had continued to improve overnight and I wouldn't have to worry about hand-bagging her during the day. Tomorrow the Berk baby would have his hernia repair and circumcision. I wondered what the bris ceremony would be like and whether we'd be able to participate.

I was not on call that night, so I stopped by our fellows' office to drop off my jacket and change into scrubs. I had worn "real clothes" as we called them, because I had a date that night. Then, I made my way up to the NICU and found Dave, the fellow who had been on call the previous night. Thankfully, he said, the baby girl had been great, weaning on both the ventilator and the meds we had her on. A set of 30-week twins had been delivered by C-section because their mother had developed pretty bad hypertension and swelling (preeclampsia), but they were doing well on fairly low ventilator settings. All in all, a good night in the NICU.

After rounds, I started going around the unit, examining babies and talking to the nursing staff and parents. When I got to Baby Berk's incubator, I discovered his mother sitting there, quietly reading from what looked like a religious book and murmuring words in a language I didn't recognize. I introduced myself as the new fellow on service and she smiled and took my hand, introducing herself as Rona Berk. She said I certainly looked different than the husky, bearded doctor—David something?—who'd been on service before me. I laughed and then told her how much the staff had appreciated her bringing that box of pastries all the way from L.A. She started telling me about the bakery and then her school and finally, her shopping trip to Loehmann's. And she reached down into a shopping bag and pulled out several of her purchases for me to see. She was almost giddy with excitement as she pointed out one bargain after another.

After I'd admired the clothes she'd bought for the baby—and her shopping acumen—I began to talk about him: how his feedings were going, his As and Bs, and of course his hernia repair, which was set for the following day in the operating room upstairs. I wasn't telling her anything really new but she listened intently and asked lots of questions, most of them geared toward when he would be ready to go home with them—to southern California. Would he be able to fly? Would he need a monitor? I answered her questions as best I could; the actual discharge date would of course depend on the baby—on how quickly he recovered from his operation, learned to nipple all his feedings, and remembered to breathe.

"Are you absolutely sure now that he's going to make it?" she suddenly asked me. I hadn't been prepared for that question and it took me aback.

"Well, of course, as sure as we can be," I said. "There are always risks with any operation, but the risks are really tiny when your baby has done so well."

She must have noticed the startled look on my face, because she quickly responded. "I know that question must have sounded strange, at this point in his life, but I just had to ask it. My husband is flying up today so that he can be present for the bris we're planning to have tomorrow. Did you hear about it?"

I told her that Jeff, the baby's intern, had told us something about that on rounds yesterday, and she then proceeded to fill me in on some of the details of the ceremony. She quietly assumed the role of teacher, and I became her student.

"Usually the naming ceremony is done right after the bris," she explained, "but in this case, the circumcision will be done by the mohel, working with the surgeon in the operating room, right after the hernia repair. So the mohel says we can have the naming ceremony before the bris. We'll just do the ceremony backwards and he'll get both his English and his Hebrew names before he goes upstairs. Normally, the bris is held when the baby is eight days old. The first seven days of life represent the physical world of creation. When a child has lived for eight days, he has transcended from the physical to the metaphysical and it's time to seal the covenant. A bris has no meaning when it's performed before the eighth day of life. In our case, the seven days have been stretched into seven weeks and we think he must be ready. Still, we'd like to hear from you that you're really convinced he's going to live."

I once again reassured her, and then I realized that not once in the 15 minutes that we'd been talking had I thought about, or had she ever mentioned, her terminal cancer. She closed her book, which had sat open in her lap while we talked, and rose slowly from her chair. She needed some air, she said. As she walked away from me, I noticed how very thin she was, except for her bulging abdomen, and how slowly she moved. I wondered whether she was in pain.

I went through the day's activities in slow motion, attending a couple of deliveries, leading a discharge conference with two excited parents of twin preemie boys, and giving a short lecture on inguinal hernias to the residents on my team. All the while, I kept thinking about what Rona Berk must be going through and how on earth she was dealing with it.

It was a relief to sign out the unit to another one of my colleagues and to go out to dinner with Erik, the man who was to become my second husband. I did not discuss the Berk baby and I tried not to even think about the past few days' events that evening. There were times when it was very important to separate my professional from my personal life, and this was one of those times. Several months before, on one of our first dates, Erik had told me that he had heard that the famed San Francisco cable cars would be shut down for two years for a complete overhaul. Even though I knew he was a reporter and therefore had access to all sorts of information before it ever hit the presses, I thought he was pulling my leg. How could they ever shut down one of the biggest, if not *the* biggest, tourist attractions in the city? So, I had made a bet with him that he was wrong; I thought he was making it all up. It was to be the first in a long series of wagers that I would lose with him. Those cable cars did shut down, amazingly, and were down for two full years. But at least I had bet Erik something that I, too, could enjoy—dinner out at his choice of restaurants. That night, we enjoyed a very elegant dinner at one of the most expensive restaurants in the city. It cost me nearly two weeks' pay.

When I walked into the unit the next morning, I was momentarily startled to see a solemn group gathered around the area near Baby Berk's bed. At first, I was alarmed. Could something bad have happened to him overnight? Then I realized that it must be the bris, or at least the naming ceremony. Of course, I should have realized that since his hernia repair had been scheduled for nine o'clock, the ceremony would have to begin earlier in the morning in order to get him upstairs on time. There were several bearded men wearing black suits and white yarmulkes, one of whom had his hands on Rona's shoulders as she sat in a rocking chair, holding her son. I assumed that he was her husband and one of the other bearded men must be the mohel. Both looked like my idea of a rabbi.

The NICU quieted down as the ceremony got underway. Several of us watched from a respectful distance. One of the bearded men sat in a chair that had been placed next to Rona and she handed him the baby to hold in his lap, with the monitor leads still attached. I learned later that this man was the baby's uncle and was the honored *sandak*, the person who would have held the baby during the actual bris or circumcision. Prayers were murmured, songs were sung, and the baby emerged with two names—Joshua, his English name, and Yehoshua, his Hebrew name. And his monitor didn't go off once. *Mazel tov!*

Later that morning, after Joshua had been in the operating room for about an hour, I was called upstairs to attend a delivery. The operating room used for our neonatal surgeries was the same one used by the obstetricians for cesarean sections, and so it was right next to the delivery rooms and our resuscitation room. The residents and the NICU staff and I were discussing what we knew so far about the delivery we'd been asked to attend, which was a full-term baby with a suspected spina bifida. We were all talking at once as we stepped off the elevator but we immediately stopped our chatter when we saw Rona Berk, sitting in a chair outside the operating room, quietly saying prayers from a book she held in her lap. I saw that her face was tear stained and she was dabbing at her eyes with a small handkerchief. I quickly went up to her and asked her whether everything was okay in the operating room. Had she been given any disturbing news from the surgeon? And she said no, everything was fine. The mohel had just finished doing the bris with the surgeon and told her that Joshua would be coming out soon.

I didn't have to ask her why she was crying. Now I knew. Her firstborn son had just had his first important Jewish ceremony, and it was likely the last one she would attend.

CHAPTER 11

Christopher

To some parents and most hospital staff, Christmastime in the NICU is too depressing for words. I used to feel that way, too, because Christmas is my favorite holiday and I wanted to be home—baking cookies, decorating the house, wrapping gifts, attending Christmas Eve mass—and not at the hospital. But one day, I took care of a very tiny baby in the delivery room who changed the way I viewed Christmas.

He had no name at first. His parents, Sophia and Dan, had been planning, trying, hoping, and praying for his birth for nearly 10 years. When Sophia found out she was pregnant, she was afraid to hope that it would last, that she would one day really have a baby. But when her obstetrician told her that the baby would be due on Christmas Eve, she suddenly felt relieved and hopeful. How could anything go wrong now? Her due date seemed like such a good omen.

And for the first few months of her pregnancy, it was. She had never felt better; she didn't even have a twinge of nausea. Her baby was growing well and so was she, having gained 10 pounds in just four months. Sophia didn't mind a bit when she began bursting through the seams of her jeans. After all, she was eating for two now, and she was thrilled when her pregnancy began to show. She and Dan had waited until she was 12 weeks pregnant to tell their family and friends. They'd already endured six miscarriages during which their hopes were suddenly dashed and others' congratulations were replaced by consoling hugs, tears, and too often, silence. But none of those pregnancies had ever gotten beyond 12 weeks. It seemed to them that that was the magic turning point.

At 18 weeks, Sophia felt really and truly pregnant and through the miracles of modern medicine, she had managed to stay that way long enough for it to be noticeable. She allowed herself, finally, to read *What to Expect When You're Expecting* and she savored every single word, holding herself back from reading the next chapter until she'd actually achieved that gestational age landmark. She just didn't want to jinx it.

Sophia and Dan knew that they were at increased risk for having a baby with a genetic disorder because of Sophia's advanced maternal age. They had started trying to get pregnant shortly after they were married, when Sophia was 30, but now, 10 years later, she was 40 years old. Their perinatologist (high-risk obstetrician) had counseled them regarding their risks and told them that certain blood tests and ultrasound findings could provide a better estimate of those risks. But if they wanted something more definite than a risk estimate, they could opt for genetic testing, such as an amniocentesis or chorionic villus sampling. There were risks to the pregnancy from these procedures, and Sophia and Dan were terrified. How could they take a chance on losing this pregnancy, now 10 years in the making? They weren't even sure what they would do if the test results indicated that their baby had Down syndrome. Could they really terminate their pregnancy because the baby wasn't going to turn out right? Happily, the blood tests and the ultrasounds suggested that the risk for a genetic disorder was low, and so Sophia and Dan decided not to have any genetic testing done. Later, they told me that they were so glad they'd made that decision. They would have felt so guilty at the thought that in choosing to have an amnio, for instance, they might have caused what eventually happened.

One day, in late September when Sophia had just reached the 24th week of her pregnancy, she was planting some bulbs in her garden when she suddenly felt a strange wetness between her legs. She had been kneeling on her garden pad when the pressure on her bladder from her growing uterus had made her feel as though she needed to go to the bathroom. *Oh well*, she thought, a bit embarrassed. *I must have just had an accident.* She went inside to shower and change her clothes, and it was then that she noticed that the fluid in her panties had streaks of blood in it. "Oh my God!" she exclaimed, as she slowly realized what had happened. She had broken her bag of waters. It couldn't be true; it just couldn't. Not after everything they'd gone through to get this far. She started feeling the contractions as she was dialing Dan's work number.

At the hospital, the news was not good. Her amniotic membranes had ruptured, and now she had developed a fever and her white blood cell count was high. Infection inside the amniotic cavity was suspected. There was no point in trying to stop her labor. The baby would likely be born that night. Although the fetal heart rate monitor already showed signs of fetal distress, a cesarean section was not recommended by their obstetrician. The baby had only a slim chance of survival, and these grim odds would not be improved by doing a cesarean. Furthermore, when a cesarean was done so early in a pregnancy, when the uterus was very thick, a "classical" incision was needed, which meant that she could never have a vaginal delivery and that her uterus could rupture during another pregnancy. Their obstetrician recommended that the couple speak with a neonatologist, and that's when I first met Sophia and Dan.

I was the neonatology fellow on call in the unit that night, and this was one of three prenatal consults I'd been asked to do.

A labor room loaded with high-tech equipment and heavy with fear and anxiety is hardly the best setting for offering detailed medical information, or for waxing philosophical about the ethics of neonatal care at the "limits of viability," to parents of a very premature infant. The essential information, which is all that is usually remembered afterward, includes some estimate of the baby's chance for survival and, for the survivors, the odds that he or she will be "normal." At 24 weeks' gestation, the chance of survival at our hospital in the early 1980s was 10 percent at best, and the majority of the survivors were left with major handicaps such as blindness, hearing loss, mental retardation, and/or cerebral palsy. "Saving" such extremely premature babies was, and still is, considered experimental by many neonatologists. There was a lot we could do to resuscitate and to care for these babies, but the question was always whether we should. The wishes of the parents mattered. But what could I tell them that would allow them to make a truly informed decision regarding the care of their baby at the time of delivery?

I took a deep breath and walked into the room. I surveyed the controlled chaos that was typical for an impending high-risk delivery. Sophia was lying on the hospital bed in the center of the room, hooked to IVs, catheters, and monitors. Her cheeks were flushed and her forehead was beaded with sweat. Three hours earlier she was a healthy, glowing pregnant woman working on her garden, thinking about what to cook for dinner. Now, she'd suddenly become a patient—a scared, sick patient in grave danger of losing her baby. Her husband sat close by her side, holding her hand. Neither of them looked at her exposed abdomen with the fetal monitor belt wrapped around it, glistening from the jelly applied earlier for the ultrasound to check the fetal size and position and the amount of amniotic fluid remaining. Instead, they had their eyes glued to the monitor screen where they watched and heard their baby's heartbeat. Their baby was still alive.

I walked up close to Sophia's bed, positioning myself so that both parents could see me without shifting their positions. Someone—I can't remember who—had told me never to sit on the bed. There's so little privacy in a hospital room, and a patient's bed is the last vestige of it. I introduced myself as a pediatrician who specialized in taking care of babies—especially premature babies. And I told them I was there to give them as much information as I could about their baby's chances, should the baby be born now. Like so many parents in similarly tragic situations, they were glad to see me. They were so hopeful that they'd now be hearing some good news.

I always start my prenatal consults with two questions: first, what do you know about premature babies? And second, what have you been told so far about your baby? These questions were designed to get the parents talking and also to give me a chance to know how they've processed any information they may have already heard or read. In answer to the first question, Sophia told me that she had a cousin who'd had a premature baby—at 32 weeks. He had been on a respirator for a few days but now seemed fine, at a year of age. And she also said she'd read about a set of quadruplets in *McCalls* magazine. They'd been more premature than her cousin's baby, she recalled, and one of them had died. Dan said his mother had told him that he had been born about a month early and had stayed in the hospital for two weeks until he could eat. In answer to the second question, Sophia said that the obstetrician had told them that if the baby was born now, there was only a slim chance of survival, and that he therefore wouldn't think of doing a C-section. They both looked at me expectantly.

First, I told them that there were preemies and then there were preemies. All preemies had essentially the same problem—they were just fine until they were born too soon, before they'd finished growing and developing. But her cousin's baby, born at 32 weeks' gestation, was so much farther along than their own baby that there was virtually no comparison between them. Yes, they'd face similar difficulties with lung, brain, and intestinal development. But the degree of difficulty of each problem was exponentially higher at 24 weeks' gestation for every single organ, including the largest organ in the body, the skin.

"So then, what are his chances?" Sophia whispered.

"Do you already know it's a boy?" I asked.

Dan volunteered that during one of their fetal ultrasounds, a technician had pointed out something that was unmistakably male—at least to him. Dan gave me a brief, proud smile at that recollection.

"Babies born at 24 weeks' gestation are so immature that they usually don't survive," I began. "Even if we can get them past the first few days of severe lung problems with our special baby respirators, injuries to the brain, intestines, skin, and other organs can be so severe that they just don't make it. And boys, especially white boys, seem to have the toughest time of all. In answer to your question, Sophia, if your son is born today, I'd estimate his chance of survival to be around 10 percent."

I paused to let this sink in and to gauge their reaction. For most people, hearing that there's a 10 percent chance is the same as hearing there's no chance at all. Yet others hear it quite differently: there's actually a chance they'll take their baby home. They hear it as "1-in-10 odds," which sounds so much better than one in a hundred or one in a million, or never. I watched Dan squeeze Sophia's hand tighter as tears rolled down her hot, flushed face. Their reaction seemed like most people's. I'd just confirmed what their obstetrician had told them, which was very bad news.

I wasn't surprised when Sophia then asked me what his chances would be of being "normal" if he was one of those rare survivors.

"It's a lot harder to predict the risk for handicap than it is to predict survival," I explained. "We know today exactly how many babies born at 24 weeks' gestation died here last year or the year before. Most die within the first days or weeks of life, so those statistics are about as up-to-date as you can get. But for things like mental retardation, cerebral palsy, or even learning disabilities, you have to wait until those kids get old enough to test them. That may not be until they reach age two or even school age. And you have to follow a reasonable number of these babies in order to be able to say anything meaningful about them as a group. And then you have to publish your results in a medical journal, which can take up to a year. So, the bottom line is that any information on how surviving 24-week infants do in the long run is based on the outcome of babies who were born about 10 years ago."

With that caveat in mind, I explained to them that the published information we had indicated that the majority of 24-week survivors were handicapped; often, multiply handicapped—with vision and hearing problems, as well as cognitive and motor impairments. But, I added, it's important to realize that there are many different *degrees* of such handicaps. For example, some preemies with cerebral palsy are so mildly affected that only a developmental pediatrician and their parents could tell, while others are so severely affected that they're unable to sit without support or walk. And cerebral palsy did not always come with mental retardation, as many people assumed.

Now came the moment of truth. I had been in Sophia's room for about 30 minutes. Her contractions, which I could see on the monitor and in the grimaces on her face, were beginning to intensify. I guessed that we were going to see their baby—their fetus—within the next few hours. I needed to tell them that they had some say in what we did or did not do for their baby in the delivery room.

"I'm so sorry to be the one to give you such grim statistics," I began. "Although what I just told you are just statistics—and they don't tell us with any real certainty what's going to happen with *your* baby—they can help us make choices. There's so much we can do to try and save preemies, beginning in the delivery room. But just because we can do all these things doesn't mean that we should, especially if the chances of a good outcome are so poor."

"What are you saying?" Dan asked.

"Loving and caring parents, like yourselves," I replied gently, "sometimes decide, before their baby is born, not to begin any high-tech medical interventions such as putting the baby on a respirator or starting CPR if the heartbeat is slow. When parents have made that decision ahead of time, our team is still there when the baby is born. But instead of doing all of our high-tech resuscitation procedures, we begin what we term 'comfort care.' We would quickly assess the baby's condition, dry and warm him, and then give him to you to hold."

"Oh my God! Please stop!" cried Sophia, as a strong contraction began. I didn't know whether she meant my words or her contractions, or both. Dan gripped both her hands until the contraction passed. For a few minutes, neither of them looked at me. You could have cut the air with a knife.

Then, Sophia turned to me and asked, "Is there anything in between doing nothing for him and doing everything? I don't think I could ever forgive myself if I didn't give him at least a fighting chance. But I don't want him to suffer because of us, just because we want him so badly." And then she added, "Did you know his due date is Christmas Eve? That just has to mean something hopeful, don't you think?" Tears rolled slowly down her face. Dan looked stricken.

These are the kind of prenatal consults that are so incredibly hard emotionally. I had to talk to the parents at one of the worst, perhaps *the* worst, moments in their lives. I had learned not to put myself into their shoes, though. If I did, I just couldn't get through it without breaking down myself. And they needed someone to be professional and somewhat objective.

"Well, yes," I replied after a heavy pause. "There is an approach that we term the 'trial of life,' which in a way is something between comfort care and an aggressive 'do everything' approach. We basically see how the baby responds to life outside the uterus, while we gently stimulate him and give him some breathing support with a bag and mask. If he doesn't respond at all to these initial interventions—no movement, no breathing, still blue, and no increase in his heart rate—then it's unlikely that any more aggressive procedures would help in the long run. In a way, he would be making the decision for us. On the other hand, if he responds in some way—moving, crying, breathing, increasing his heart rate, and turning pink—then we could go ahead and put him on a respirator, put catheters into his umbilical cord vessels, and admit him to the NICU."

They both looked at each other and then turned to me and said, nearly in unison, "That's what we want."

My pager went off and I glanced at the message. It was the NICU, and there was a "911" next to the unit number. That meant they needed me over there—now. I apologized to Sophia and Dan and told them I really had to run, but I'd be able to come back if they had more questions. No, they said; they understood what I'd told them and what would happen when their baby was born. "We trust you," Dan said, "to make the right decisions, but you have to know that we both hope and pray that he passes that—what did you call it?—trial of life."

As I bolted from the room, I called out, "I hope I don't see you again for several weeks." I always said that, but in this case, I certainly didn't believe it. And I doubted that Sophia and Dan did, either.

My stat 911 call was about a baby in the NICU who'd "blown a pneumo"—the baby was very tiny and had terrible lung disease, so she was on pretty high ventilator settings. This proved too much for her fragile lungs, and one lung literally popped so that the air going in leaked into the pleural cavity lining it. As the leak increased, so did the pressure on the lung until it simply collapsed. Premature babies do not do well with only one lung. When I'd finished draining the air and supervised the resident putting in a tiny chest tube hooked up to a gentle vacuum, I sat down to write my prenatal consult note. A written summary was needed in Sophia's chart so that everyone who took the time to read it would know what the resuscitation plan was for the baby. And then my beeper went off again, this time to the delivery room—also with 911 attached to the number. There were so many sick babies in the NICU that day that I decided to leave the resident there and to attend this delivery without her in tow.

Jessie, the unit's charge nurse, quickly grabbed the DR "tackle box," which was in fact a real fishing tackle box that we kept filled with all the equipment and drugs we would need for a high-risk delivery. We took the stairs up to the delivery room with Mike, one of the respiratory therapists, following closely behind.

"Do you know what it is?" shouted Jessie as we ran.

"I have a pretty good idea," I replied. "I bet it's that ruptured 24-weeker that rolled in this afternoon."

"Have you had a chance to talk to the parents yet?" wheezed Jessie at the top of the stairs. That was the big question. What did they want us to do?

I called back to her, "They want us to see what happens and take it from there."

"That's just great," Jessie gasped. "Leave it up to us." But I knew that wasn't what Sophia and Dan really meant. They just didn't want to be the ones to make, and to live with, the Big Decision—

did their baby live or die? Far better to have the baby "declare himself" and then ultimately for someone else, like me, to make the final choice.

As soon as we got to the labor deck, we made a beeline for the Crisis Room. That's what we called the room where we carried the sickest babies right after birth. There were two warming tables set up in there with all the equipment we could possibly need to resuscitate just about anything, right at each of the tables. As Jessie and Mike busied themselves getting things ready at one of the tables, I poked my head into the adjacent delivery room and sure enough, there was Sophia—looking ready to deliver—with Dan by her side.

"Jessie," I said before I went into the DR, "could you please make sure someone calls the attending?" We fellows stayed "in house" round the clock and could manage pretty much everything, but the birth of babies at the limit of viability, like this one, warranted the presence of the attending neonatologist, too.

I then went into the DR to touch base once again with Sophia and Dan. I took hold of Sophia's free hand (the other was tethered to her IV) and reintroduced myself, in part because I was now wearing a mask. "Oh, Dr. Gleason," she said. "We are so glad you're here. We're just hoping so much that he makes it."

Those words "makes it" made my heart suddenly squeeze inside my chest. Of course they wanted him to live. How could they not? And even though I knew that the risks were enormous if he made it out of the delivery room, in a way I wanted to go for it, too. It was always easier to just go ahead and *do* something and see what happened than to decide *not* to do anything, knowing that then the baby would surely die.

I assured Sophia that I would take my cues from the baby and that I would do the best I could. I pointed to the swinging door connecting the delivery room to our Crisis Room and said that

I'd be taking the baby in there, and that Dan could join us if he wished.

"No, no, I want to stay here with Sophia," he said abruptly. "She'll need me more. And what can I do in there anyway?" he said bitterly, pointing to the Crisis Room.

Fathers like Dan were really in a terrible position. The birth of your first child should be such an incredible, life-changing experience. Fathers always talk about that amazing moment when they held their newborn and looked into his or her eyes for the first time. But here was Dan, already feeling helpless and torn between his new baby and his wife. I told him that I'd try to keep them both informed as events unfolded.

As I returned to the Crisis Room, my OB counterpart, the perinatal fellow, came over to me and whispered, "We've heard that the parents haven't made any decision about the baby."

"Well, that's not exactly right," I replied. "They've opted for the 'trial of life' approach; basically, we'll see how he responds to some basic resuscitation steps and then we'll take it from there."

"So you're not going to intubate him?" he queried.

That was always the crux of it. Do you intubate or not? Intubation of the trachea, followed by placing the baby on a respirator in the NICU, was the Code word for "doing everything." We might wind up intubating him, I explained, but only if he responded in some way to our initial efforts.

I glanced around the room and could see that Jessie and Mike had everything ready to go on the table closest to the delivery room door. Suddenly the swinging door to the DR flew opened and someone shouted, "This is it." I quickly glanced at Jessie, one of our most experienced NICU nurses.

"It's showtime," she said quietly as we both went into the DR to be ready to "catch" Sophia and Dan's tiny baby.

The DR staff could tell that delivery was imminent because now you could see that the baby's head was crowning. In other words, the top part of his head, the crown, became clearly visible every time Sophia pushed with her contractions, looking like a shiny red Christmas ornament.

"Can you see his hair?" Sophia gasped in the space between her contractions. Not yet, someone said, although the reality was that he had no hair. He was too early.

And then, with the next contraction and push, he came flying out. This tiny human, the size of a pound of butter, was quickly cut from his placental lifeline and placed on the warmed blanket I had draped over my outstretched hands.

I held him up very briefly so that Sophia and Dan could have a quick look at him, and said, "Congratulations. You have a son." No matter how tragic the circumstances, and no matter what happened next, this was after all an incredible moment for Sophia and Dan, which it seemed important to acknowledge. They were now officially parents.

And then I headed for the Crisis Room through the door that Jessie held open for me. The adrenaline level was very high in that room, especially in me. The attending had not yet arrived.

I put the baby down on the warmer. His eyes were fused shut, like a kitten's, and his skin looked like cherry Jell-O. He smelled like rancid butter, a telltale sign of chorioamnionitis, the intrauterine infection that likely was responsible for his premature birth. He would begin losing enormous amounts of water and energy through his gelatinous skin if we didn't prevent it somehow. Jessie quickly put a piece of *Saran Wrap* over him, leaving just his tiny head exposed. The plastic wrap would allow us to see his movements and to use a stethoscope on his chest. Jessie also cut a small opening in it, over his umbilical cord, and pulled the cord through it. In these tiny babies, it was often easier to count faint heartbeats by feeling the pulsations in the umbilical cord than to try and hear them with a stethoscope. Jessie also stuck tiny needle electrodes in both his upper arms and thighs. The regular skin monitor leads just didn't stick on skin like his.

A heartbeat pattern appeared on the monitor screen, which I could also feel in his umbilical cord. His heart rate should have been about 150 beats per minute but was about 80. Still, he was alive even though he just lay there, motionless. We gently stimulated him by moving his legs and rubbing his chest, being very careful with his skin. Nothing happened. He didn't move and his heart rate remained low. Only three minutes had passed since his birth.

"Should I bag him?" asked Mike, the respiratory therapist. He held our smallest facial mask in his hand, attached to a ventilation bag through which some oxygen was flowing. Jessie and I looked at each other. This wasn't the Big Step—intubating him—but it was a step forward nevertheless. And if he didn't respond to bag-and-mask ventilation, Mike would be asking whether I was going to intubate him.

"Don't you want to weigh him first?" Jessie asked me. Sometimes it was easier to decide to forgo resuscitation if you knew the baby weighed less than a certain amount; say, 500 grams.

"No, let's just go ahead and bag him," I decided. "I told the parents we'd do the basic things and see how he responds, and I think bag-and-mask ventilation qualifies as basic."

I didn't add that it would also potentially give me more time to assess him and to make these terribly difficult clinical judgments. Only a few minutes had passed since he'd been born, but it seemed like an hour. I needed more time, and so did the baby.

Mike started bagging him, although at first he had trouble getting the mask to fit snugly, with a tight enough seal over his tiny mouth and nose. Once he got a good seal, we began to see his tiny chest move a little each time Mike squeezed the bag. It didn't move much, though, even when Mike squeezed harder. His lungs were already pretty stiff. It was quiet in the room as we all listened to the heart rate monitor. Jessie had set it so that you could hear each beat as well as see the pattern on the screen. The baby's heart rate slowly began to rise and his color started to turn a bit pinker, but he didn't move. He didn't try to take a breath or cry.

After a couple of minutes, the baby's belly started to fill up with the air being bagged in. Mike stopped bagging for a minute while Jessie fed a small catheter from his mouth to his stomach and sucked out some air, which temporarily deflated his belly. The only way to get the air from the bag into his lungs, and only his lungs, was to intubate him. It was also getting harder for Mike to keep a good seal on the mask and to move air into those stiff lungs. And the baby still hadn't moved or responded in any way to our efforts except for a modest increase in his heart rate and some improvement in his color.

We all looked at each other. Should I go ahead and intubate him or not?

"He's so immature," said Jessie, pointing out the obvious. "Look at his fused eyes and his Jell-O skin. I'll bet he's less than 24 weeks."

She was right. I looked again at this tiny, still human and I knew he didn't stand a chance. And yet, could I really predict his outcome? After all, he was born alive and we'd been able to keep him alive without too much effort so far. Hadn't he passed the "trial of life"? And there was so much more we could do for him in our NICU. But I also knew that if he lived, he'd be so likely to have significant brain damage and numerous other complications of extreme prematurity—and to suffer in the process. Is that what his parents wanted? They'd tried for so many years to have a baby; he was likely to be their last hope of having one of their own. Should we get more aggressive with his resuscitation or not? Should I let him live or die? How could I possibly make such a wrenching decision?

And then it happened. The baby made the decision himself. His heart rate suddenly decreased and Mike couldn't move his chest at all. Blood began oozing from his mouth and nose. His tiny lungs must have ruptured—a pneumothorax—and he was likely having a pulmonary hemorrhage. I sighed audibly, mostly with relief. We all looked at each other; no one had to say anything. It was clear that there was nothing we could do for him except keep him comfortable and bring him to his parents.

Mike stopped bagging him and Jessie took the stomach catheter out of the baby's mouth and removed the tiny needle electrodes from his arms and legs. She gently cleaned his mouth and face and removed the *Saran Wrap* blanket, replacing it with a warmed cotton one. And she selected a cute blue knitted hat from a big bag of them and placed it over his bald little head. The hats were knitted by a group of devoted elderly ladies who brought in a bagful at least once a month. All of our NICU babies wore those hats at one time or another, graduating to a normal baby-sized one when they finally went home. I was glad that Sophia and Dan's baby had a chance to wear one, too.

Jessie wrapped the little guy in a blanket and handed him to me. I held him next to me for a moment, imagining what this would feel like if he were my baby. Tears welled up in my eyes. It was just so sad, thinking of how hard these parents had tried to have a baby and that this was how their journey into parenthood was going to end.

I wiped the tears from my eyes with the cloth diaper Jessie had handed me to use to keep the baby's face clean. Bloody secretions were still oozing from his mouth and nose. I needed to look and act professional when I brought Sophia and Dan their son and explained what happened, and somehow, my tears didn't seem appropriate.

I walked into the DR and saw Sophia sitting up on the bed, all cleaned up and ready to move to a postpartum room. Dan was at her side, still holding her hand. They looked up at me expectantly and then they saw the bundle in my arms. And they knew.

As I placed the baby in Sophia's arms, I briefly recounted those first few minutes of his life: how he had been born with a heart rate and had briefly responded to our efforts, although he'd never moved or tried to cry. And then how he'd suddenly deteriorated, which we suspected was caused by his lungs just being too immature.

"He's such a beautiful baby boy, perfect in every way," I told them. "You really grew him well, Sophia. He was just born too early."

Tears streamed down Sophia's face as she held her son tightly to her. "Is he still alive?" she asked me.

"Yes, his heart is still beating, and it may continue beating for a while," I told her. Even though I wasn't sure that was true, I didn't want to put a stethoscope on his chest or feel his umbilical cord just to find out. I knew it would be important to them that their son died in their arms.

"But he's not feeling any pain," I assured them both. "Nature takes care of that with the high carbon dioxide level that he has now. That will put him to sleep better than any anesthetic."

Holding her newborn son tightly to her chest, Sophia was wheeled into her postpartum room, which thankfully was private. Sophia and Dan held their son for hours, well after I'd listened to his silent chest for a full minute and pronounced him dead. They undressed him and counted all his tiny fingers and toes and gazed at his little backside. They studied his face to see who he resembled more and they took lots of pictures. And they named him Christopher. Not a family name, they said, and certainly not after me. They named him Christopher because he was supposed to be their Christmas baby and they wanted to remember and commemorate that forever.

And they did just that. I was on call in the NICU on Christmas Eve that year, and I was sitting in the staff lounge, listening to Christmas carols and feeling depressed and sorry for myself. Then, the door flew open and Jessie appeared, holding a huge gift basket filled with goodies and a big bag filled with red felt Christmas stockings—more than enough for every baby in the NICU.

"You'll never guess who brought all this stuff," Jessie said. "Do you remember that 24-weeker who died last fall? Well, his parents said he was supposed to be born tonight and this is how they wanted to remember him."

I ran out into the hall and saw them waiting for the elevator. Dan carried another huge gift basket in his arms, this one destined for the obstetric staff. As I walked toward them, Dan put down the basket and they both came and wrapped their arms around me.

"This was supposed to be his birthday," Dan explained. "We've had Christmas Eve in mind ever since they told us it was our due date. It seemed like such a good omen at the time." He looked so sad for a moment, but then he brightened. "We decided that this was his other birthday, his *real* birthday, and we couldn't think of any place other than here at the hospital where we'd rather celebrate it."

"Thank you for everything you did for Christopher and for us," Sophia said. "We wish more than anything that we still had him with us, no matter what problems he had. But we're so glad that he made the decision for us and that we could be his parents, even if it was for such a short time."

I didn't have to tell them how glad I was, too, that their baby had taken that terrible, wrenching decision away from me. Death was always hard to take, even when it was expected, but death with uncertainty or guilt was the hardest of all.

CHAPTER 12

Erica

"Now I just make a small cut in the vessel with the spring scissors, like this," said Dr. Rudolph, in his quiet, measured South African accent, "and then I use the forceps to gently lift up the vessel and introduce the catheter." I watched in awe as he slipped the tiny catheter into the even tinier blood vessel, and he did this despite a hand tremor, which seemed to worsen as he got closer to his goal. I was one for ten on successful placement of this particular catheter over the past year—and that one was just dumb luck as far as I was concerned. Dr. Rudolph never missed.

I was now in my second year of neonatal fellowship training and was receiving this lesson in catheterizing the tiny portal vein of a preterm fetal sheep from my research mentor, Dr. Abraham Rudolph. One of the requirements of neonatology fellowship training was to demonstrate "meaningful accomplishment in research" by the end of the three-year training program. Like most brand-new fellows, I hadn't done any basic research, let alone anything meaningful, and I worried about that aspect of my fellowship training much more than the clinical training. When I knew that I'd be going to San Francisco for my neonatology fellowship, I had decided to work in Dr. Rudolph's lab because I'd been told by his son Colin, who was a medical student in Cleveland while I was a resident, that it was the best fetal physiology lab in the country. Colin had also told me that his father was a masterful teacher—and I knew I'd need a master if I was to accomplish anything meaningful.

Dr. Rudolph was a pediatric cardiologist and had used a chronically catheterized fetal sheep method for many years to investigate all sorts of important physiological questions. Basically, this involved doing a cesarean type of operation on an anesthetized pregnant ewe. Various parts of the fetal sheep would be brought out through an opening in the uterus so that catheters could be placed in blood vessels and various monitors and equipment could be inserted into or around the fetus. Anything we placed into the fetus or the amniotic cavity would be "tunneled" under the ewe's skin so that the ends would come out of a cloth pouch that was sewn onto her flank. Finally, we'd close all the surgical incisions—I got much more practice putting in stitches in the sheep lab than I ever had during my surgery rotations—and the fetus and ewe would come out of anesthesia and generally behave as though nothing had ever happened. A few days later, when we were sure that both ewe and fetus had completely recovered, we'd have an incredible window through which to study normal fetal life or fetal responses to changes in its environment.

My research project involved looking at how glucose was made by the fetal liver, both before and after birth—a process called gluconeogenesis. When Dr. Rudolph first told me about this project, I thought it was an odd area for a cardiologist to be studying. But when he told me that no one else in the lab was working on the project, I decided to plunge in, even though I had no burning interest in, and very limited knowledge about, fetal liver gluconeogenesis. I figured that I would have Dr. Rudolph's undivided attention and tutelage, which also included the attention of his research assistant,

Christine. When I started working in the lab in 1982, Christine had already been working with Dr. Rudolph for about 15 years. I quickly came to realize that she was vital to the lab's success and national reputation. Dr. Rudolph and other investigators had the brilliant research ideas and designed the experiments; Christine made sure it all happened. Most of the time, I operated on the fetal sheep with Christine. As the fellow/trainee, I was expected to put in all the catheters myself, with her assistance. But I hadn't yet mastered the portal vein catheter technique, so Dr. Rudolph was usually scheduled to scrub in when we got to that critical part of the surgery. I'd try a couple of times to get the catheter in myself and then Dr. Rudolph would bail me out.

Christine took a personal interest in the lives of all of the trainees and investigators in the lab. We all looked forward to operating with her or doing long experiments, because we'd get a chance to talk with her about our professional and personal problems. Over the pregnant belly of many an anesthetized ewe, we had long conversations about such things as my feelings of incompetence in the lab (as compared to the NICU); a difficult transport I'd managed; a baby who died after weeks in the NICU; and my 1981 divorce and growing relationship with a writer for the *Wall Street Journal*.

Today was no exception. After Dr. Rudolph successfully placed the portal vein catheter and left the operating room, I started telling Christine about my frustrations with a biochemical assay that I needed to develop in order to measure new glucose production by the fetal liver. I'd been working on it for months, fumbling along with biochemical pathways I hadn't really thought about since medical school, mathematical equations, plastic compound separator "columns," and glass scintillation vials that were placed in gamma or beta radioactivity counters. Once I got the assay working, I'd be able to determine whether the fetal sheep liver was capable of gluconeogenesis, or making new glucose. It sounded simple enough, but it wasn't simple at all. And it had to be as close to perfect as I could get it, or the results of all my studies wouldn't be valid.

"The thing is," I complained to Christine, "it's so hard to see the clinical relevance of all this work I'm doing. It's so far removed from the babies I'm taking care of in the NICU. I mean, who cares if the fetal sheep liver is capable of gluconeogenesis?"

"You must always keep the big picture in mind, Chris," said Christine emphatically in her heavy Peruvian accent. "You might not see the direct relevance of your little piece of research now, but together, all the little pieces could solve a bigger problem that could help a lot of those little babies."

I knew Christine was right, of course. Where would we be in neonatology if it weren't for the collective research efforts of countless numbers of investigators toiling away on their little projects? But still, I longed to work on a research question that I'd actually asked while working in the NICU. We spent the rest of our operating room time together discussing the latest gossip in the lab as well as my upcoming weekend trip to Mendocino with Erik, my *Wall Street Journal* boyfriend. We'd scheduled the trip, our second one to the same bed-and-breakfast, for this coming weekend because I was starting another one-month rotation in the NICU on Monday. We both knew we wouldn't see much of each other during that rotation.

The weekend was intense — as was our relationship at that point. I didn't think about the lab, my fellowship, or gluconeogenesis for one minute. We got back late Sunday afternoon, driving through the fog on the Golden Gate Bridge in my orange Dodge Dart Swinger. We were both lost in thought — me with the beginnings of what I'd taken to calling "the dreads," that feeling I always got before I went on service. I'm not sure what Erik was thinking, but I had a pretty good idea. Our relationship had taken a serious turn toward commitment, and he was probably feeling both elated and petrified.

After I dropped Erik off at his Nob Hill apartment, I drove over to the hospital to meet John, the fellow signing out the service to me. No rooftop bar handoff tonight, because John was in-house covering the unit. He knew that I was returning from a weekend out of town, and he'd prepared a detailed handoff sheet for me so that we could spend the least amount of time going through the kids on our service. It took him only 30 minutes to hit the highlights, which was a good thing, as I suddenly realized how tired I was.

The last baby on John's list was Erica Dougle, a one-week-old 26-week gestation preemie who'd had a pretty rocky course so far. She had the usual preemie lung problems and was still on a ventilator. And now she had all the signs of a significant ductus—a heart murmur, fluid retention, and worsening lung disease. The ductus arteriosus is a normal fetal blood vessel connecting the aorta, the artery carrying blood from the heart to the body, with the pulmonary artery, the artery carrying blood from the heart to the lungs. In the fetus, the ductus allows the nice pink blood coming back from the placenta to bypass the fetal lungs after it goes through the fetal heart. There is no need for blood to go to the lungs because the fetus isn't breathing. After birth, the ductus is supposed to close because the placenta is gone, the baby is breathing, the pressure in the lungs goes down, and now, blood does need to go through the lungs and get pink before it goes out to the body. In a full-term infant, the ductus naturally closes within the first day of life. In preemies, though, it stays open, and this allows too *much* blood to course through the lungs, flooding the lungs and making the baby sick. Surgical closure of the ductus—literally, tying it off—used to be the only option if the baby got very sick. And then an amazing discovery was made. You could give a premature baby aspirin or indomethacin, which is an aspirin-like drug, and the ductus would close.

"We're planning to start indomethacin on her tomorrow," John explained, glancing at his detailed list. "But her urine output has never been great and we're worried about her kidneys, so we've ordered some blood tests for the morning. If her creatinine level is really high, you'll have a difficult decision to make." John and I both knew that babies treated with indomethacin often had a decrease in their urine output, and sometimes stopped peeing altogether. The open ductus itself contributed to their kidney problems, because blood that should have been going to the kidneys was sidetracked and went to the lungs instead. But indomethacin affected renal function too and sometimes, the combination of a wide-open ductus and indomethacin shut the kidneys down completely. Jimmy, the first preemie I'd cared for during my residency, suddenly popped into my mind. We'd tried indomethacin to close his ductus and when that hadn't worked, we'd sent him to the operating room for surgical closure—and he died several days later.

I said good-bye to John, telling him I hoped he would have a good night—for his sake and for mine—and headed home to my Point Lobos apartment. A long hot shower, a grilled cheese sandwich, and a glass of wine would help to ease the "dreads," which had intensified since I'd gone around the unit with John. Unpacking my weekend bag could wait.

The next morning, I caught the 38 Geary bus and headed for the hospital. I arrived a bit earlier than I'd expected, so I had time to get a hot cup of coffee from the coffee shop around the corner. I headed upstairs to the unit and, as always, the "dreads" disappeared as soon as I walked into the room. I spotted John in the far corner, near Erica Dougle's incubator.

"I had a great night," he told me. "No deliveries; no admits; and no one crashed."

We both agreed that his great night on call was great for me, too. It was definitely more difficult to come on service when the unit was in chaos as compared to when it was just quietly humming, as it was this morning.

"Dougle's creatinine is 1.8," John informed me. He'd been checking the morning labs, which had been drawn and sent by the night nurses earlier, around 5 A.M.

"Wow, that's really borderline for giving her indomethacin," I said, not telling John anything he didn't already know. Normally, the blood creatinine level in a preemie, an indicator of how well the kidneys were working, was lower than 0.5. A preemie with an open ductus often had a higher creatinine, perhaps up to 1.0, primarily because the kidneys weren't getting as much blood flow. We really worried about the kidneys when it was higher than that, and we used a cutoff of around 1.5 to decide whether to start indomethacin or not.

"Ron Clyman's attending this month, right?" I asked John, knowing that in the end, this would be an attending decision. Ron was the research director of our fellowship training program. But more relevant to Erica Dougle's creatinine was the fact that his own lab research, for which he had a national reputation, was focused entirely on the ductus. He'd created a newborn lamb model in which he could regulate whether the ductus was open or closed, and he studied many ductus questions—such as how it closed naturally and how indomethacin really worked.

"Yup, you've got Ron for the whole month, starting today," replied John. "And I seem to recall that the last time I was on with him, he let us give indomethacin when the creatinine was less than 1.8, but I could be wrong."

As John headed out the door on his way home, I was briefly wistful, knowing that I had a whole month of clinical service ahead of me and he was done, for now anyway. Then I turned to my clipboard and got down to work, filling in the rest of the morning labs and chatting briefly with Jen, the pediatric resident on the service, before rounds started at eight o'clock. These rounds went more slowly than they should have, because all of us were new to the service—me, the attending, and the pediatric resident. Usually, changes in service were staggered by at least a day so that some-one knew what had been going on with the patients, but for some reason that hadn't worked out this month. It wasn't until 10 o'clock that we reached Erica Dougle's incubator and Jen began to present her brief history and her current problem list—which she listed by organ system. She saved the cardiac system for last, since it was the one she knew we'd need to spend the most time discussing. I watched Ron Clyman listening carefully as Jen described Erica's worsening lung disease, her higher oxygen needs, her generalized fluid retention, and her borderline kidney function—including the latest serum creatinine value.

"She's becoming a little puffball," said Jen, and we all peered through the clear incubator walls to observe her puffy eyelids and her sausage-like little hands and feet.

"How much effect do you think the open ductus has on her kidney function, Chris?" asked Ron.

"A lot," I replied quickly. "Blood that should be going to her kidneys is being directed instead to her pulmonary circulation," I said, more for Jen's benefit than to show off my own knowledge.

"Then how much effect do you think the indomethacin would have on her kidney function, independent of the ductus?" Ron asked me next.

I gave the party line regarding indomethacin; that is, I knew that kidney blood flow and urine output usually decreased after one or two doses were given to a preemie to close the ductus. But I didn't really know how to gauge the interaction between the ductus and the drug or the timing of these interactions.

"If the ductus started to close due to the indomethacin, then kidney function should improve, right?" prompted Ron. "The ductal closure could sort of cancel out the negative effects of the indomethacin—unless there was something intrinsically wrong with her kidneys in the first place."

I was getting a little impatient with Ron at this academic discussion. Erica's creatinine was elevated and the question was, should we treat her ductus with indomethacin and risk kidney failure or just send her to the operating room for a surgical ligation, and risk all the complications of surgery? There wasn't a good way for us to test the independent effects of the ductus and indomethacin on a preemie's renal function. We'd just have to make a clinical decision and then see what happened. But Ron was a master at bedside clinical teaching and we spent another 10 minutes discussing every aspect of kidney function, the ductus, and indomethacin—complete with several diagrams drawn on paper towels showing different blood flow and urine output responses.

In the end, Ron left the final decision to me. "Well, what's it going to be, Chris?" he asked.

I felt my hands go clammy and my chest tighten. Despite that extended academic discussion, I realized how limited the information we had to make this important decision was. Remembering Jimmy, my first preemie, and the hazards of surgery in tiny preemies, I took a deep breath and said, "Let's go with a course of indomethacin."

And so we did. Jen ordered the customary three doses of the medication, to be given every 12 hours. We cut back the fluid we were giving the baby, because we knew she'd have a decrease in her urine output, and we ordered daily follow-up tests of her serum creatinine levels for the next three days.

Erica received her first dose of indomethacin at noon. Soon afterward, the NICU suddenly got much busier with two admissions from the delivery room and one admission transported from a regional community hospital, a baby with a diaphragmatic hernia.

Babies with that particular birth defect were usually very sick because some of their intestines had herniated from the abdomen into the chest through a hole in their diaphragm, crowding out the lung on that side and pushing the heart against the lung on the normal side. But fortunately, this baby was amazingly stable; in fact, the problem had been picked up by an astute pediatrician on his discharge physical who had discovered that the baby's heart sounds were heard best on the right side of his chest instead of on the left, and he'd gotten a chest X-ray to figure out what was up.

The resident and I had lots of admission notes and orders to write, so it wasn't until midnight, when we walked around the unit to check on all the babies, that we found out that Erica had not produced a single drop of urine since she'd had that dose of indomethacin at noon. She looked puffier than she had on morning rounds and when I listened to her with my stethoscope, I could still hear her ductal murmur. This wasn't surprising, because it usually took a couple of doses of indomethacin to close the ductus, but I was hoping that it might have worked faster in Erica. Now we had a dilemma. Should we give her the second dose of indomethacin, which she'd clearly need in order to close the ductus, even though she was temporarily in renal failure? Or should we hold off and wait for her to start peeing, knowing that at that point, the indomethacin would be less likely to work? Her nurse had sent a creatinine level to the lab just before we'd started our midnight rounds, and I called the lab to see if they had a result. It wasn't good; Erica's creatinine was up to 2.0.

I decided I'd better call Ron, who was the attending on call that night. This was fortunate for me, because I wouldn't have to go through all the details we'd discussed on morning rounds with a new attending.

After I'd explained the situation, Ron asked me, as I knew he would, "So, Chris, what do you want to do?"

I was torn. What if we gave her the second dose of indomethacin and her kidneys completely shut down and never recovered? It was a possibility, although I'd never actually seen it happen. On the other hand, we couldn't send her to the operating room for a surgical ligation right away—because of her renal failure—and that meant she'd have to continue struggling with that open ductus, which of course wasn't good for her kidneys. The question was the same one we'd addressed on morning rounds: Which was worse for her kidneys, the indomethacin or the ductus? Again, I thought of Jimmy.

"I think we should go with the second dose and hope that it closes her ductus," I said, with considerably more certainty in my voice than I felt within me.

So Erica Dougle got her second dose of indomethacin at 1 A.M. And for an agonizing three days, she did not pee. Not one drop. We cut back her fluids to the bare minimum—just enough to keep her hydrated—and still, she got puffier and puffier until she looked like the Pillsbury Doughboy. Her creatinine kept rising: 2.5, 3.4, 4.8, and finally 6.1. I'd never seen a preemie with a creatinine that high who'd recovered. It was a very bad sign.

We'd put in a tiny bladder catheter through her urethra so that we'd know instantly when she started to make some urine. Several times each day and during the nights when I was on call, I'd check that catheter to see if there were any "golden drops" visible in the tubing. Sometimes I'd even press on her suprapubic area to see if I could make her pee. Nothing.

We needed to turn up the rate and pressure on her ventilator as she got bigger and bigger and the excess fluid in her body spilled over into her lungs. Her oxygen needs went up too, so that finally she reached the maximum—100 percent. The only positive thing was her ductal murmur: the day after I ordered that second indomethacin dose, it had disappeared.

"So if her ductus is closed, why aren't her kidneys getting better?" I asked Ron on morning rounds on the third day after that second dose, as we all stared gloomily at her "flow sheet," where the column under "urine output" had only zeros. After all, this was what I'd based my clinical decision on. In my judgment, the ductus was worse for her kidneys than the indomethacin. That's why her creatinine was so high to begin with, I'd reasoned. But if I was right, then since her ductus had been closed for at least 48 hours, we should have started to see some improvement.

Ron didn't have a good answer to my question; clearly, he'd agreed with my judgment or he wouldn't have allowed me to make either of the treatment decisions he'd asked me to make.

Later that day, I walked by Erica's bedside and took yet another look at her catheter. And then I looked again. Could it be true? Was there actually some urine in the tubing? I could barely contain my excitement as I called her nurse to confirm this amazing finding. She quickly came over and peered closely at the little catheter while I pressed on Erica's suprapubic area. We both looked at each other with huge grins on our faces, and shouted in unison, "She's peeing!!!"

And so it was that Erica Dougle's kidneys came back to life. Shortly after I saw those first few drops, she began an amazing flood of urine, the so-called post-ATN (acute tubular necrosis) diuresis. When failing kidneys recover, they initially overshoot the mark, basically excreting everything that comes their way. We let Erica pee these huge volumes for a full day before we started slowly replacing some of the enormous fluid volume she was losing. Our little puffball "de-puffed," as we sometimes put it, so quickly that I didn't recognize her when I saw her two mornings later after being off for the night. Within just a few days, she was literally half the size. It was such a relief to the whole NICU team—and especially to me. I had felt ultimately responsible since I'd made the decision to treat her ductus with indomethacin instead of surgical ligation.

As the month wore on, and I began to wear out, I couldn't stop thinking about Erica and that whole question of ductus versus indomethacin. Neither could Ron Clyman, as it turned out. He began telling me about a newborn sheep experiment he'd been considering for the past year. Working in Dr. Rudolph's lab, where I was examining fetal liver gluconeogenesis, he had created a model in which he could close the ductus of a newborn sheep or make it stay open. He had also figured out a way to resuscitate and stabilize premature newborn sheep on the ventilator, just like we did with preemies in the NICU. And Dr. Rudolph had developed ways to measure newborn renal blood flow and function. Putting all these methods together, Ron had the idea that he could give indomethacin to a newborn preterm sheep, with or without a ductus, and then measure the independent effects of either the indomethacin or the ductus on the kidneys — and of course, the combined effects as well.

It sounded like a brilliant idea to me, and I realized why Ron had developed such an outstanding reputation as a physician scientist. It also seemed like such a clinically *relevant* experiment, especially when compared to my fetal gluconeogenesis experiments. I was thrilled when, at the end of the rotation, Ron asked me if I wanted to participate in his new experiment. I thought about it for, oh, a minute maybe, and then said yes — as long as I could work out the timing with my other experiments and sheep surgeries. This turned out to be no problem at all. Ron and Christine would operate on the fetal sheep, placing the ductus controller and all the catheters we'd need to use after the fetus was delivered. Then, on the day of the actual experiment, the fetus would be delivered by C-section and resuscitated with all the things we customarily did for preemies. It would take several hours to get things stabilized before we started the actual experiment, so I could work on my other lab projects in the morning and early afternoon and then join the team (Ron and Julio Perez-Fontan, a pediatric intensivist) as the actual experiment got underway. Ron would determine which protocol we would follow for each sheep—indomethacin or not, ductus open or closed, or some combination of these. And then the experiment would begin—ending 12 hours later.

Twelve hours was a long time to spend in the lab, taking care of a preterm sheep and waiting to make various measurements every few hours or so. We talked about politics, books, and occasionally, medicine. We listened to music, although we each had completely different tastes. We smuggled in a tiny TV and watched *M*A*S*H* and *Jeopardy!*, and someone usually went out to get something to eat around dinnertime. Ron was married to a Frenchwoman who was an excellent cook and he had refined gourmet tastes. Julio liked spicy Mexican foods. But my favorites, for which I received endless ribbing, were burgers and fries from the nearby fast-food places.

My contribution to the experiment was to do the renal function tests and blood flow measurements and in the end, to analyze the data and write the manuscript. It was an amazing experience as I began to see, as the results of our experiments came together, that my clinical judgment about Erica had been correct. While indomethacin did have negative effects on newborn kidney function, it was the ductus itself that had the more negative effect. And in fact, the worse the ductus problem was, the worse indomethacin's side effects were—which is probably why Erica's renal function had deteriorated so badly after the drug was given. Her ductus had been so large and it had been open for a while, wreaking havoc on her kidney function, and it was just as her kidneys were ready to quit that we'd given her the indomethacin.

I needed to keep reminding myself, as I wrote that manuscript for the *American Journal of Physiology*, that a newborn preterm sheep is not necessarily the same as a preterm human infant. But by learning so much about this vexing clinical problem in an animal model,

I somehow felt that my clinical judgment was bound to be the better for it. I couldn't wait to get the manuscript published and to share this little piece of scientific knowledge with other neonatologists. For the first time, I appreciated the great potential of medical research—although I personally remained ambivalent about my own abilities to actually do it and do it well.

CHAPTER 13

Anna

I T WAS JUST as expensive to live in San Francisco in the early 1980s as it is today, especially on a fellow's salary. I paid $585 each month to rent my one-bedroom apartment on Geary Boulevard plus $25 a month for a garage space in the apartment building (a must because of the late hours I kept), about $50 a month for food, $15 a month for a MUNI bus pass, $10 a month on gas—those were the days!—and $120 a month on my medical school loan. When I began the fellowship training program in 1982, my salary before taxes was $15,500 a year. When I added up all my expenses and realized my take-home pay would be only $1,100 a month, less than I'd taken home as a resident in Cleveland, I knew I'd need to find a moonlighting job if I wanted to do anything besides eat, sleep, and get to and from the hospital. Plus, although I still loved wearing clothes I'd worn in high school, they did wear out, and, as Erik gently reminded me, they went out of style—badly in some cases.

Fellows weren't supposed to moonlight because the extra work could tire us out, detracting from our educational experiences. But the faculty knew we all did it (except for one fellow who was known to have "family money") and they just looked the other way. They knew we had to earn some extra money if we were going to have a life. So, during my first month in San Francisco, I asked the senior fellows where they moonlighted and one of the cardiology fellows told me that a spot had opened up at St. Luke's, one of the community hospitals in town. It was an ER job. St. Luke's had a moderately busy emergency room that didn't see enough pediatric patients to justify hiring a full-time pediatrician, so they did the next best thing—they hired moonlighting pediatricians to see pediatric patients during the busiest shifts (generally evening and night). I'd finished my pediatric residency and was eligible to take my pediatric boards, so I was a full-fledged pediatrician even though I was still in a training program.

After a brief interview with the medical director of the St. Luke's emergency room, I was hired. I was expected to do two 6-hour evening shifts and one 12-hour overnight shift per month, on average. During those months when I was on service in the NICU, they knew I wouldn't be doing any shifts at St. Luke's but that I'd make up the shifts on one of my research months, when I didn't have as much clinical call. I would be paid an amazing $50 an hour—just what I needed to stay afloat financially in San Francisco.

At first I was nervous about functioning as a "real" pediatrician but after a couple of shifts, I relaxed. The adult ER docs were very experienced and could and did handle just about anything. They'd help me with lacerations, especially those on the face, and they'd set all the broken bones, something I had never learned to do as a pediatric resident. Mostly, I saw kids with coughs, colds, ear infections, and stomach ailments—typical pediatric ER fare. Parents would often just hit the wall with their baby's screaming or their kid's incessant coughing—especially late a night. They didn't want to bother their pediatrician or sometimes they didn't have one, and the ER was always open. The evening rush usually began after five o'clock when Dad returned home from work and could manage the household while Mom took the screaming baby to the ER. I did sympathize with those exhausted, frazzled mothers, but it wasn't until I had children of my own that I really knew the depths of despair you reach when you just can't stop a baby's crying or a child's coughing—especially at three in the morning.

One gray, rainy day in February, I arrived in the ER to start a 5 P.M.–to–11 P.M. shift. It would be my last one for at least a month, because I was scheduled to start a rotation in the NICU the following Monday. As I was stowing my coat, purse, and battered copy of *Handbook of Pediatric Emergencies* in a locker in the charting room, the ER medical director told me that he had scheduled a medical staff dinner meeting for six o'clock. Could I cover the adult patients, too, for two hours or so, so the adult ER doc could attend? I agreed to do it as long as the adult doc remained nearby in case a real emergency came in, such as a heart attack or stroke victim.

I was finishing up with a baby who had "the squirts," meaning diarrhea, when Randy, the adult doc, poked his head in the exam room and said he was leaving for the meeting.

"I've written my pager number on the whiteboard in the charting room, Chris," he said, "and the meeting is just down the hall. Call me if you get a real sicko, okay?"

I assured him I'd call him for anything more than I thought I could handle and off he went. I saw a couple more pediatric patients—a toddler who'd fallen down the stairs and a teenage girl with a bladder infection—before the triage nurse gave me the chart for my first adult patient. I glanced briefly at his "chief complaint," which the nurse had scrawled at the top of his chart: "Cough." *You've got to be kidding*, I thought to myself, as I walked into the exam room. There, sitting on the exam table, was a man who looked about my age, dressed in business attire, coughing and blowing his nose into a nice-looking handkerchief.

I tried hard not to be judgmental as I introduced myself and got down to business. "I'm Dr. Gleason," I began. "And what brings you to the emergency room tonight?"

Looking slightly annoyed, he answered, "Haven't you seen my chart? I caught a bad cold a couple of weeks ago and I'm still coughing. It's driving me crazy. I need something to stop it."

I just couldn't keep myself from asking him, "But what's the *emergency?*" It was one thing to deal with a mother who'd had it with her child's incessant cough. But a grown man?

The guy looked even more annoyed as he answered, "I needed to see a doctor about this cough and this ER is open 24 hours a day. Do you know how long it would have taken me to get an appointment with my doctor? And what do you care anyway? You're paid to see anyone who walks in the door."

I sighed. Better to just get on with the exam and give him a prescription for something than to start arguing with him about his inappropriate use of the ER. The rest of his history was unremarkable—no wheezing, shortness of breath, night sweats, weight loss, or coughing up blood—which meant I could more or less rule out asthma or tuberculosis, or something even worse, like cancer. And his exam was fine. I heard nice, clear breath sounds and no wheezing when I put my cold stethoscope on his chest. He had no ominous rashes or lumps in his neck or under his arms. The only positive finding was a little redness in his throat, which was most likely due to irritation from his cough.

"You've got a mild case of bronchitis," I explained. "The lining of your bronchial tree became irritated with your cold and it's just going to take some time to get better."

"Don't you need to get an X-ray and order some blood tests in order to be sure?" he asked, clearly disappointed that I hadn't come up with something more serious.

No, I explained, X-rays and blood tests weren't necessary, based on the results of my exam and the fact that he had no fever or other signs of something serious.

"Well, what are you going to give me for my cough, then?" he demanded, jumping down from the table and taking off his hospital gown. "Don't I need some antibiotics or something?"

"No, you don't need antibiotics, just some cough syrup you can buy in the drugstore," I told him, trying not to laugh as he stood bare chested and glaring at me. Now he was *really* disappointed.

"Thanks for nothin', doc," he snapped, throwing on his shirt, grabbing his hat and briefcase, and striding angrily out of the room.

I exchanged glances with the triage nurse as I filled in the rest of my paperwork. She assured me that the adult docs got the same treatment from some of their patients.

"Big babies is what they are," she sighed as she handed me my next chart. "Worse than some of the two-year-olds, if you ask me."

I glanced at the chart before I went into the exam room. It was a four-year-old girl whose chief complaint was "sore thumb."

A solemn, chubby little black girl named Keisha sat in her mother's ample lap. She was holding her sore thumb tightly in her other hand. Her mother explained that she'd been sick for a couple of days during the previous week with a fever. She'd gotten better but then started to complain about her "suckee thumb," as she called it. As I spoke with her mother, Keisha gradually got more comfortable with me and soon started to play with the little stuffed koala bear I had around the end of my stethoscope. I seized the opportunity to begin my exam, listening to her heart and lungs as she remained in her mother's lap. She let me look at her throat. I used one of the colorful tongue blades I kept in my jacket pocket. She even let me examine her ears, which were fine. Finally, I asked to see her thumb and she shyly held it out for me. I took her hand in mine and could easily see why it was sore. She had an angry swollen red lump along one side of her thumbnail. "Owie," she said as I gently pressed on it.

It looked like a pretty straightforward paronychia—basically, an abscess that starts under a nail—and it needed to be lanced. Letting the pus out would relieve the pressure and the pain and allow faster healing. I explained the procedure to Keisha and her mother. It would hurt for just a few seconds while I put in the numbing medicine and it would feel a whole lot better afterward. I stuck my head out the door and called for one of the ER nurses. I needed a few specific supplies and I needed someone to hold the little girl, who was not so little, while I lanced her thumb.

All things considered, the procedure went quite smoothly. Surprisingly, though, hardly any pus came out when I made a small, deep cut directly over the swollen, inflamed area on her thumb. Usually, lancing a paronychia is like popping a zit. As I bent down to look at the thumb a bit more closely, Keisha decided she'd had enough. She jerked her hand away from the nurse's hold and pushed my face away. There wasn't much more I could do anyway, I explained to her mother, as I wrote a prescription for a liquid antibiotic for her to take for the next week. After she'd put a small Band-Aid over the sore, the ER nurse put a rubber thumb guard over her entire thumb—to keep the wound clean and to keep her from sucking the thumb. Keisha was not happy about losing access to her favorite digit, which doubled as her binky, but she brightened considerably as she was led to the toy box and allowed to select one of the toys to take home. As I completed the paperwork, I briefly considered what else besides a paronychia could have been wrong with Keisha's thumb. I was glad that I'd recommended that she see her pediatrician for a follow-up visit in a day or two. Soon afterward, the ER suddenly got much busier and I forgot all about Keisha's thumb.

A week later, I was on call at night in the NICU at the end

of the first week of one of my four-week rotations there. It had been a tough one. We'd had two deaths already, and one preemie named Anna clung to life with the worst lung disease most of the attendings had seen in a long while. She'd already had four chest tubes placed in her tiny chest to treat pneumothoraces—small lung ruptures. *One week down, three to go,* I thought to myself as I lay down for an hour or so on the pull-out sofa in the fellows' office. I hadn't realized how tired I was until my head touched down on the scratchy hospital pillow. I was always tired when I was on service, but that night I felt more tired than I'd ever felt before. I worried that I wouldn't hear the phone ring or worse, be able to get up when I was needed for a delivery or for an urgent problem in the NICU. And as I lay there, I became more aware of a canker sore in my mouth that I had first noticed earlier in the day. It was more painful than my usual canker sores and seemed to be getting larger by the minute.

Somehow I fell asleep, only to be awakened abruptly an hour or so later by the jarring ring of the phone, which I'd placed right next to my head. I felt dizzy, feverish, and disoriented as I dragged myself from the bed and upstairs to see Anna, who had suddenly turned blue again. The resident thought she'd had another pneumothorax and as I looked at the X-ray, my heart sank as I realized he'd guessed right. Despite two chest tubes draining extra air from each side of her chest, she'd accumulated more, and that extra air was pushing hard on what remained of her poor little lungs. I decided that it would be useless to put in a fifth chest tube. There just wasn't any room for another one, I thought, as I looked at her tiny chest wall. Tubes and monitor leads covered nearly every available inch. I decided instead to reposition one of her existing tubes, choosing the one closest to the extra air visible on her chest X-ray. This was definitely a job for a fellow, not the resident, eager though he was to do the procedure. Fellows had a lot more experience with chest tubes, and manipulating one that was already in place wasn't something that was easy to teach.

I ordered an extra dose of morphine for Anna and put on a sterile gown. She was feeling the effects of that pneumothorax more now; her heart rate was starting to drop and her color was awful. Luckily, she wasn't in an incubator, which would have limited our access to her during the procedure. The respiratory therapist could stand on one side of the warming table she lay on, "bagging" her by hand, while I worked on the other side. I decided to get on with the procedure, forgoing the surgical hat and mask and just putting on sterile gloves. Later, I was to anguish over and over again about that decision.

My hands were shaking, and so was I—from fever and chills as it turned out—as I undid the dressing over that chest tube and then cut off the tiny stitches holding it in place. I directed the resident to turn the baby slightly into different positions as I moved the tube back and forth and up and down. It was connected to the suction machine, so we could all see when that extra air suddenly shot back through the clear tubing. Everyone was relieved when Anna's heart rate immediately rose and she gradually pinked up, or at least returned to her more typical, slightly blue color. I'd succeeded, evacuating that extra air without putting in a fifth chest tube, temporarily stabilizing her so that we could at least put her back on the ventilator.

Usually, I felt a warm, wonderful inner glow when I'd done a procedure well. But as I sank into one of the padded rocking chairs next to Anna's bedside, I felt awful. It was all I could do to scrawl a brief procedure note in her chart. I knew I should call her parents to let them know what had happened, but I let the resident do that. My mouth was killing me now, not just where that canker sore was, but all over. It was too painful to talk.

I sat in that rocking chair for the rest of the night, dozing on and off and feeling sicker and sicker as the night went on. Luckily, Anna remained stable as that repositioned chest tube continued to bubble with extra air. And there weren't any high-risk deliveries that the resident couldn't handle on his own.

By morning, I knew that I'd have to go home. I was too sick to work. One of my fellow colleagues would have to replace me. That would be a first. Somehow, I'd always managed to work through colds, laryngitis, even "the crud"—which all pediatric residents had at least once during their training. But this was different. I felt so bad that I actually considered going directly from the NICU to the ER or at the very least, seeing a doctor. Except that I didn't have one—which wasn't at all unusual for medical trainees like me.

After I'd signed out, I did ask Phillip, the NICU attending, to look at my mouth before I left for the day. By now, it felt as though all my gums were disintegrating and I could hardly swallow. I knew that Phillip had been a practicing pediatrician for a few years before he became a neonatologist. Maybe he'd seen something like this before. He whistled through his teeth as he peered inside my mouth with a flashlight, using a tongue blade to gently move my tongue out of the way.

"It's really bad, Chris," he said solemnly. "Looks like some kind of viral infection. Could even be herpes. You'd better see a doctor."

"Herpes?" I mumbled in a daze. "How would I get oral herpes?"

I knew all about genital herpes, of course, but I personally didn't know anyone who had it. As neonatologists, we always worried about babies getting herpes from their mothers' genital herpes lesions as they were being born. Herpes infections could make babies very sick, especially if the babies were premature, and sometimes they died. Oral herpes causes cold sores, and babies can also acquire herpes from cold sores and be just as sick. But somehow it was less of a concern for us than genital herpes and besides, unlike genital herpes, you could easily see when someone had oral herpes because the person would have a cold sore. Parents and staff were always required to wear a mask and practice good hand-washing whenever they had a cold sore. I couldn't think of anyone I knew or had had contact with who'd had a cold sore. Later, I realized that I'd forgotten something I'd learned in medical school. The first time you get a herpes infection, whether it be genital or oral, you don't have the typical lesions, like a cold sore. Those only come with recurrent secondary infections.

I don't remember how I got myself home that day. I do remember that by late afternoon, I realized that my mouth was so sore that I hadn't been able to eat or even drink anything all day. When you have a fever and can't drink any liquids, you can get dehydrated pretty fast. I decided I really did need to go to the ER, at least for some IV fluids, and also to find out what I actually had. I called one of the nurse practitioners who lived in my neighborhood, and she drove me back to the hospital and stayed with me while I waited the usual hour or two to be seen. My mouth was cultured, and I received a liter of intravenous fluid to rehydrate me. The ER doc said it really did look like herpes, and he gave me some liquid erythromycin—an antibiotic that he said would hurt like hell when I swished it in my mouth but would then somehow dull the pain for a few minutes so I could drink something. Where could I have acquired this infection, I asked? He shrugged and said I'd probably never know. And then he asked me a very interesting question. He knew I was a doctor. Did I ever see any young kids in my practice? And if so, had I recently seen a kid with a sore thumb?

Keisha! That little girl in the St. Luke's ER. Could she have had herpes on her thumb? Was that why no pus came out when I lanced it? I described her thumb and what I'd done with it and asked the ER doc, "Do you think she could have had herpes?"

The ER doc nearly busted up laughing as he exclaimed, "You lanced a herpetic whitlow!" He went on, reminding me of something I should have remembered from my pediatric clerkship in medical school. When kids had their first case of primary oral herpes, they'd have a febrile viral illness with a sore "throat" or mouth—just like I had now, only it's not as bad in kids. Cold sores, if they wound up getting them, would crop up later, as the herpes virus came out of hiding. Kids who were thumb suckers during that primary illness would pop that thumb in their little mouth and herpes would settle in, making a sore that looked just like a paronychia, but wasn't. I remembered Keisha's mom saying that she'd had this viral illness a few days before she'd noticed her sore thumb. That must have been Keisha's primary herpes infection. And her sore must have been a herpetic whitlow. We were taught that you didn't lance those because it didn't do any good. She had just an inflamed thumb, not an infected one.

Suddenly, I remembered how Keisha had pulled her thumb away after I'd lanced it and then pushed my face away with her hand. That must have done it. If my mouth culture came back positive for herpes, then that's how I'd probably acquired it. Still, knowing how I'd gotten it didn't make me feel any better.

I spent the next week in bed, as sick as I'd ever been in my life. Periodically, I'd swish that erythromycin antibiotic around in my mouth and after a minute or so of searing pain, my mouth would go numb and I'd be able to swallow some liquid—only water at first, and then gradually some soda pop. I lost 10 pounds from my 110-pound frame and started feeling like a swizzle stick. The ER phoned with the results of my mouth culture; it had come back positive for oral herpes. So it was true. I'd probably gotten it from my misdiagnosis of Keisha's sore thumb.

As I hung up the phone, I suddenly thought about Anna, the baby with the pneumothoraces that I'd been up most of the night with on my last call night. Oh my God, I thought, could I have given her herpes? I remembered how I hadn't had time to put on a mask before I'd repositioned her chest tube. And had I washed my hands really, really well before I put on my gown and gloves? I lay there drenched in sweat, some of which was from my fever and some from a terrible anxiety that had suddenly set in. I knew that the incubation period for herpes was one to two weeks, so I wouldn't know whether Anna had gotten herpes from me for at least that long. But a "high index of suspicion" was needed; that is, the people caring for her needed to know that she'd been exposed so that they could consider herpes if she took a major turn for the worse. There was a treatment available, but it wasn't very effective if you started it too late into the illness. I had to call the unit right away and let them know what I had.

I talked to Dave, the fellow who'd come out of the lab to take over for me. "It's really herpes," I said, and before I could stop myself, I started to cry. "I'm so worried that I exposed some of the babies in the unit when I was on call that night," I sobbed. "Especially Anna, that kid with the terrible lung disease and all those chest tubes."

Dave reminded me that it's very difficult to transmit herpes by hand-to-hand contact—it's usually caused by contact between one mucus membrane, such as the mouth, and another mucus membrane. But then I told him how I thought I'd gotten herpes in the first place. And we both knew that I wouldn't breathe easy until at least two weeks had passed and no one in that unit had been diagnosed with a herpes infection. Then we talked about the babies in the unit, including Anna, who was still there, but as unstable as ever. Dave related how he'd had to replace one of her four chest tubes the night before because it had stopped working and she'd gotten another pneumothorax. That poor baby, I thought, suffering so much, and for what? If she survived these first few weeks and finally got those painful chest tubes out, she'd probably develop terrible chronic lung disease and eventually die from that—still on a ventilator and in 100 percent oxygen.

One night during that difficult week, Erik came over and made me some soup—from scratch. Very impressive, and even more so because our relationship was "on the skids," as we called it, at that point in time. A few weeks earlier, after an intense "commitment" conversation that didn't go well, we'd somewhat mutually decided to date other people for a while. That soup was probably delicious, but it was tomato soup and as I took a sip, we both realized too late how acidic it was. Despite a vigorous pre-sip erythromycin swishing, it just killed my mouth. Still, that tomato soup and Erik's effort in making it brought us closer together somehow, and led, I believe, to our getting engaged—the first of several engagements, though of course neither of us knew it at the time.

By the end of that week, I was able to drink liquids without first swishing my mouth out with erythromycin and I was starting to eat some soft foods. My fever had gone and I was definitely on the mend. Dave kept me posted on the kids in the unit—no herpes so far, although everyone by now was aware of the potential exposure. Any time a baby developed signs of infection, a herpes culture was added to the septic workup that was routinely done. Dave and I decided that he would finish the last three weeks of my aborted four-week rotation in the NICU, and then I'd come back and work for three weeks when he was supposed to have come on service. That would give me plenty of time to recover and maybe even get some work done on the research paper I was writing.

One morning, about two weeks after I'd gone home from the unit, I woke up and took a shower and then started brushing my teeth—something I'd been able to do only for the past several days. And a very weird thing happened: I started drooling toothpaste and water out of the left corner of my mouth. I tried taking another swig of water and swishing it around my mouth and the same thing happened. I peered into the mirror and noticed that the big crease around the left side of my mouth looked less prominent and sort of droopy, compared to the right side. And when I tried to shut my eyes tightly, my left eye stayed partially open. It hit me suddenly: I had what's known as a Bell's palsy—the left side of my face was partially paralyzed, as if I'd had a stroke. Erik had spent the night and I ran into the kitchen, where he was drinking a cup of coffee and reading the paper.

"Do you notice anything funny about my face?" I asked.

He looked at me quizzically as I opened and shut my mouth and tried to squeeze my eyes shut.

"Well, it looks a bit lopsided, especially when you try to shut your eyes," he said, "but it's not really something I would have noticed if you hadn't asked me to look."

That's a relief, I thought, hoping that Erik wasn't just being charitable. Even though I felt as though the left side of my face was just hanging there, all slack and flabby, at least it wasn't that obvious to him. I got out my internal medicine textbook from medical school and turned to the page on Bell's palsy. Sure enough—one of the suspected causes was the herpes virus, which apparently liked to hide out in the facial nerve. Lucky me! First this dreadful herpes infection, and now a facial palsy. I just hoped it wouldn't get worse, and above all, that it wouldn't be permanent.

A week later, my Bell's palsy was still there, but at least it hadn't gotten any worse. I'd learned to brush my teeth without toothpaste and water dribbling all over my chin, and I could eat and drink, slowly, without anyone suspecting that there was anything wrong. About the only thing I couldn't do—at least not very well—was to play my clarinet. I temporarily suspended the clarinet lessons I was taking at the San Francisco Conservatory. It had been three weeks since I'd left the NICU that morning, and it was time for me to go back to work and let Dave go back to the lab. I'd been so relieved when the two-week point passed and no babies had been diagnosed with herpes, not even Anna.

This time, Dave and I sat at the rooftop bar at the Sir Francis Drake Hotel, sipping our Manhattans and doing our, by now, traditional NICU sign-out. Anna wasn't the sickest patient on the list anymore, but she was the one we spent the most time talking about. As we had all feared, she had developed severe chronic lung disease. All her chest tubes were out, but her over-inflated little lungs looked like Swiss cheese on her chest X-rays, full of cysts and scars. Now four weeks old, she was still on high ventilator pressures and she spent most of the time breathing 100 percent oxygen, which barely kept her pink. There wasn't much we could do to improve her dismal prognosis, except perhaps give her steroids. Steroids were powerful anti-inflammatory drugs, but we didn't like to use them because they impaired growth—especially brain growth and development—and they made babies more susceptible to infection. But when babies had such bad chronic lung disease, steroids were sometimes miraculous. They sometimes turned things around so dramatically that we could, at least temporarily, decrease the high ventilator pressures and the amount of oxygen—both of which were damaging to fragile, developing lungs. Dave told me that the team had had a long talk with Anna's parents the day before and everyone had agreed that despite the risks, she should be started on dexamethasone, a powerful steroid. I was so relieved that I hadn't given her herpes. Steroids would be the last thing you would give to a baby with an infection, especially a herpes infection, because the drug impaired the already fragile immune system.

It was great to be back in the NICU the next day, although my face still sagged a bit and I had gained back only a couple of the pounds I'd lost. When we got to Anna's incubator on rounds, I marveled at how she'd grown and how much better she looked without all those tubes sticking out of her chest. And then her nurse pointed to the oxygen dial on her respirator. We were all amazed to see that she needed only 30 percent oxygen and was pinker than when she needed 100% oxygen. Her ventilator pressures had been turned way down, too—about half what they'd been the day before. No one had ever seen such a dramatic response to steroids. On rounds, we tempered our enthusiasm by reminding the residents that this dramatic response didn't mean that her chronic lung disease had been cured. The steroid dose would need to be decreased starting tomorrow, the goal being to taper it off within a few weeks. As the dose decreased, her oxygen and ventilator pressure needs would probably go up again. And of course, we all worried about the side effects of steroids—on her immune system and her brain. But still, we all hoped that at least some of the steroids' dramatic lung effects would persist and she'd get off the ventilator and be able to grow new, healthy lung tissue. And ultimately, survive—without crippling chronic lung disease and, we hoped, without stunted brain growth.

Anna did survive. She was able to come off the ventilator one week after we started the steroids and she never had to go back on it. She was ready to go home on her due date, now four months old, still on oxygen but off steroids. She looked amazingly normal, considering her poor start in life. Her chest wall did have five wrinkled little scars on it where the chest tubes had been. At least none of them had gotten too close to her tiny nipples, where her breast buds lay in wait for puberty to begin.

Her primary nurse had paged me to let me know her discharge date so I could come in to say good-bye. Her parents had brought in a huge cake with the words *Happy Graduation Day, Anna!* written in big pink letters on the top. They let me hold her while they cut the cake and served pieces of it to staff and other parents. She wore her going-home outfit, a soft, cute little onesie with matching booties, hat, and blanket.

As I sat with her in a nearby rocking chair, holding her close to my chest, I could feel her heart beating and her chest going up and down. Although she wore a length of clear plastic tubing taped to her nose that connected her to a small portable oxygen tank, she looked like such a normal baby with her cupid-shaped mouth and her nice pink, fat little cheeks. I stroked her soft, downy little head and remembered how incredibly sick she'd been, how pessimistic we'd all been, and how much I had agonized about the possibility that I'd given her herpes. Now she was ready to go out into the real world and become someone—with any luck, the person she was meant to become and not a girl handicapped by mental retardation, cerebral palsy, or poor vision because of her extreme prematurity. But who really knew the full potential of *any* newborn baby, even the healthy full-term ones? So many things, besides what babies are born with, shape the person they eventually become. In the NICU, we just try our best to save them and avoid causing too much damage in the process.

As I gazed into Anna's startling blue eyes, I had one of those rare moments of sublime satisfaction and inner peace. I was so confident that I had made the right decision in choosing to become a neonatologist. I hugged this warm, living, breathing little human being a little tighter and hoped that I'd be able to help save many more like her.

CHAPTER 14

Harry

ARRY HAD ARGUABLY one of the worst outcomes of any baby
I've ever taken care of. But his little storm cloud of a life
also had a silver lining. He was born in a small Maryland town
during the first year of the next phase of my own personal and professional journey. After four years of medical school, three years of
pediatric residency training, and three years of neonatology fellowship training, I had qualified to become a board-certified neonatologist. And that meant I was ready to look for my first real job.

Most neonatology jobs in the 1980s were "academic" or university jobs in which you were expected to become a "triple threat": an
outstanding clinician, teacher, and researcher—with the majority of
your time devoted to research. You'd be hired as a faculty member,
typically a junior or assistant professor, in a teaching hospital affiliated with a medical school with residency and fellowship training
programs. It was usually the only way you could practice neonatology, because most of the Neonatal ICUs at that time were in
academic medical centers. There were only a few nonacademic neonatology jobs available. John, one of my fellowship program com-
patriots, had landed one in a growing group practice in Portland,

Oregon. Although I was drawn to academia—it was actually the only neonatology world I'd ever known—I found certain aspects of John's private-practice job very appealing. That's because of all the things I'd done during my fellowship training, I loved taking care of babies the most, and with a job like his, that's all I'd be doing. No teaching; no expectation to obtain federal research grants; no "publish or perish" or promotion angst. Research had proven very difficult for me. I wasn't sure I was cut out to be one of those academic neonatologists who spent 75 percent of their time in the lab—and who didn't think *that* was enough. Doing research, or medical administration, was not why I'd become a doctor, and it was not what I enjoyed the most or, at least at that point in my career, what I was good at. I didn't want my 8 to 12 weeks a year of clinical attending time in the NICU to become simply "occupational therapy" for me.

But I didn't have a lot of job choices, as it turned out. It was pretty much an "old boys' club" back then, as far as job contacts were concerned. Your fellowship program director and research mentors would hear about potential job openings at colleagues' academic divisions, and would perhaps initiate a phone call or just bring up your name at a national research conference. In 1984, when I began my search, there were relatively few good academic neonatal centers and consequently, only a few good job openings. Graduating neonatal fellows competed for the plum positions not just with each other, but with more experienced neonatologists who were ready to move up (or sometimes out). In addition to briefly considering staying in San Francisco, I was invited to look at three academic positions during that year—at the University of Southern California, the University of New Mexico, and Johns Hopkins University.

After visiting Los Angeles, Albuquerque, and Baltimore and comparing their programs with what I knew about the San Francisco program, I decided on Baltimore. I had to admit that it was partly because of the Hopkins name. *Everyone* had heard of Hopkins, and I was thrilled to even be considered for a position at such a famous and highly regarded academic medical center. The neonatology division was small, and its director, whose position I was to take five years later, was looking for someone who had research experience with fetal sheep physiology. Although the Hopkins group was focused on brain research, and I had focused on the developing liver and kidney, that didn't appear to be a significant mark against me. I knew the basic research methodology and I had demonstrated "productivity," meaning I'd actually managed to publish a few papers in medical journals. The day after I accepted the position, I found a dozen roses in front of my apartment door when I returned home from work. WELCOME TO THE GROUP, read the card. I was 32 years old and I had my first real job. And I would bring my second husband with me.

Erik and I had a relationship full of angst during those three years of my fellowship training, but in the end, we decided to take the plunge and get married. We would move to Baltimore together, with Erik leaving his job at the *Wall Street Journal* to write other kinds of things. We found a Presbyterian church in Sausalito across from the Alta Mira Hotel, which came with a wonderful Scottish minister. The church also came with a great organist who agreed to play whatever we wanted. Erik initially requested the Rolling Stones' "You Can't Always Get What You Want" as our recessional because he loved it—and didn't realize the second meaning it might have for our guests. I found a florist in Sausalito who was a warlock, a male witch. We had a low-budget wedding with a chocolate wedding cake with a wooly ram and ewe on top, representing the bride and groom. By this point, I'd become very fond of sheep, working with them so closely in Dr. Rudolph's lab.

My first attending rotation in the Hopkins NICU was during the month of September, and it was incredibly busy. The average number of admissions was 50, but I admitted 75 babies that month. They had a wide variety of problems—prematurity, birth defects, infections, home births that went badly. As I made rounds with the residents, held conferences with parents, and rushed in during the night to attend deliveries and supervise resuscitations, I felt as though I had finally arrived and was doing what I was meant to do. But I also had moments when I felt like an imposter. Those were times when it seemed as if everyone, including parents, trainees, and of course, the experienced and very judgmental nursing staff, must be thinking the same thing: Who does this woman think she is? She just finished her fellowship. What does she know? Can we really trust her to make those difficult decisions?

Fortunately, I'd had outstanding clinical training, and for the most part, I felt confident as I began practicing as an attending neonatologist. I knew what to do with the myriad of relatively common problems neonatologists faced every day, most of which arose from prematurity. Perhaps even more important, I felt that I had acquired enough skill to be able to suspect the occasional zebra, instead of the more typical horse, when I heard certain hoofbeats.

Harry, however, tested nearly all of my fledgling neonatology attending skills. We got the transport call late one afternoon after a typically busy day that month. Just like Travis, my "transport from hell" during my fellowship, he was an otherwise normal-appearing full-term baby boy who just wouldn't pink up after birth. He was already on pretty high ventilator support and 100 percent oxygen at the community hospital and still, he remained blue. His blood pressure was okay and there had been no signs of maternal infection. We all wondered whether he had a heart defect, which was sometimes an easier thing to deal with in those days than persistent fetal circulation. I'd already gone through my first death as a Hopkins neonatologist that month, and it had been a baby with PFC that we just couldn't turn around. But apparently, Harry had no heart murmur, his heart size and shape were normal on his chest X-ray, and he had normal and equal blood pressures in his arms and legs. A heart defect seemed pretty unlikely. Still, I was hoping for that because I knew that if it was PFC, I would be up all night and probably throughout the next day, trying to find something magical that would make him pink and keep him that way.

The transport team had a hard time of it with Harry, although not as tough as I had had with Travis a couple of years earlier. At least Harry had a normal blood pressure and amazingly, despite the heavy hand-bagging he was requiring, he hadn't blown a pneumothorax and so he hadn't needed a chest tube. I gathered my team—residents and fellow—around the warming table where Harry lay, as the cardiologist performed an echocardiogram. Everyone sighed audibly, though not with relief, as the cardiologist announced that Harry had no structural defects and that the only abnormality was exceptionally high pulmonary artery pressures, a telltale sign of severe PFC.

As soon as the transducer was off Harry's chest, we all sprang into PFC mode. We had a relatively routine battle plan and everyone assumed their battle stations. I was the commander, and the nurse and respiratory therapist were my sergeants at arms. All night long, I alternated between hand-bagging Harry myself, trying to find just the right settings to open his narrow lung blood vessels and trying different combinations of drugs to dilate his vessels and to artificially raise his blood pressure. I taught the residents and the fellow as I worked. We would celebrate for a few moments when Harry's blood oxygen level would suddenly rise in response to something we tried, only to have our hopes dashed as he turned blue again.

By morning, I'd pretty much exhausted both my bag of tricks and myself. Harry was relatively stable, though still not well oxygenated, so I left his bedside to use the bathroom and to get a cup of coffee. I treated myself to one of the new flavored coffees that had just been introduced into the hospital's otherwise drab and dreary cafeteria fare.

When I returned to the unit, I saw that the respiratory therapist had picked up the bag and was hand-bagging Harry again. Nowadays, we would have put a baby like him on a heart-lung bypass machine known as ECMO—for extracorporeal membrane oxygenation—hours earlier, but at that time, ECMO was just a dream being turned into a reality by a surgeon named Bob Bartlett.

The charting desk in the middle of Harry's eight-incubator room in the unit was cluttered with charts, empty Styrofoam cups, syringes, and scraps of paper. I cleared off a small area and sat down, nursing my hot cup of raspberry-flavored coffee. It suddenly occurred to me that I hadn't spoken with Harry's mother yet. And it was starting to look like we were going to lose him. I knew I should get on the phone, but I put it off for a few minutes as I contemplated what I needed to tell her, and how exactly I would do it. I felt so weary and defeated, and I hoped the coffee would lift some of that heaviness from my voice. Conversations like these were always so much more difficult on the phone.

The transport team had given us some important social information when they brought Harry in. His mother, Sara, was 19 years old and single. The father of the baby was apparently not involved. Perhaps more important, and certainly startling to most of us, was that Sara had an eating disorder—anorexia nervosa—which had been made worse by her pregnancy. When she delivered seven-pound, three-ounce Harry, she weighed only 102 pounds. And to make matters even more complicated, she also had agoraphobia, a bizarre mental health condition in which affected people, usually women, get so panicky in public that they essentially become prisoners in their own homes. I wondered how—and whether—she'd gotten to her prenatal appointments, and how she'd made it to the hospital to deliver the baby. There wasn't much more information contained in the brief records copied by the referring hospital.

I finished my last sip of coffee, dialed the number of the referring hospital, and asked to be connected with the postpartum maternity ward. When I introduced myself to the unit clerk who answered the phone and said that I was taking care of Sara's baby, there was a pause.

"I'll get her nurse first," she said. "I'm sure she'll want to fill you in."

I waited for a few minutes and had actually begun nodding off when a woman finally picked up the phone. She started by asking me whether I knew about Sara's mental health issues, and I said that I did, but that I really needed to talk to her because the baby was critically ill and we might lose him.

"She's trying to leave AMA [against medical advice]," she explained. "She just can't stand being in the hospital and she doesn't want to have to eat anything either. I've never in my life seen anyone who just had a full-size baby who's that skinny. It's so terribly sad. I'm just worried that any bad news about the baby will push her over the edge."

The same thought had crossed my mind, but still, I knew that as bad as things were, most parents imagined even worse—especially if they hadn't been given any information and couldn't see or touch their baby. I told the nurse I would be gentle with Sara but that she needed to know what was going on. And I promised to fill her in on the conversation so that she could help pick up the pieces when I was done.

I have to confess that when Sara answered her phone, I was surprised that she sounded so *normal*. I don't know what I expected but somehow, with a history of such severe mental health problems, I expected her to sound crazy—whatever that means. And Sara sounded just like every other desperately worried mother I'd spoken with. I asked her what she'd been told about Harry, and she explained that the transport team had told her that he either had a heart defect or that his lungs were still behaving as though he were in the womb. I was amazed that she'd not only heard and processed this information correctly, at probably the most stressful time of her life, but she had actually remembered it the next morning.

I first gave her what I felt was the only bit of good news; that is, Harry did not have a heart defect. I felt, rather than heard, her sigh of relief. "But unfortunately, Harry's lung blood vessels are still clamped down," I explained, "just like when he was in your womb. And we've been unable to keep them open for longer than a few minutes at a time. We're trying everything we can, but I have to be honest with you. I think we could lose him."

I hated the silence that inevitably followed a statement like that. I wanted to fill it with all sorts of hopeful things, but I knew that the bad news just had to sink in.

"Please, please try to help him," she pleaded, sobbing into the phone. And then she asked me that terrible question that all mothers ask themselves, at one time or another, when something bad happens to their baby.

"Is it my fault?"

I knew what she was referring to, and I had actually considered this possibility. An eating disorder could set up all sorts of internal problems that could affect a developing fetus, and who knew if PFC could be one such result? But I started in with my standard reassuring response.

"Every mother wonders if she did something wrong when something's wrong with her baby at birth, but most of the time it's no one's fault. Bad things happen to good people and to their babies," I said, but even as I said this, I cringed. It sounded so rote and so hollow.

I could tell she was not reassured when she asked me if I knew that she hadn't been eating properly during her pregnancy and that in fact, she hadn't gained any weight. All I could tell her was that I had known of other pregnant women who had had the same problem, and their babies had been fine—which was true. But I doubted that any of those mothers was as severely affected as Sara.

I spent a few more minutes talking with her and answering some of her questions about our treatment of her son, and then I told her I needed to get back to his bedside. Across the room, I could see and hear his monitors alarming and another respiratory therapist rushing over to hand-bag him. I promised Sara that I would keep her posted and just before I hung up, I asked her when she was going to be discharged and might be able to travel to Baltimore to be with Harry.

"I don't know if I can make it," she stated flatly. "I just need to get home and out of this hospital. Call me at home this afternoon." And then she abruptly hung up the phone.

We continued to work on Harry all through that morning and well into the afternoon. The residents and fellow who had been on call the day and night before went home, but the attending—me—had no coverage. In some ways, I often felt that we worked harder than the trainees, and I wondered then whether that was best for patient care.

Sometime in the middle of that long two-day day, Harry started to lose the battle. His blood oxygen level had dropped dangerously and acid was building up in his blood. His blood pressure started dropping and so did his heart rate. I took the bag from the respiratory therapist and tried to work magic with different rates and pressure, but nothing happened. We took an X-ray to make sure he hadn't blown a pneumothorax and he hadn't, which was amazing after all that vigorous hand-bagging. He was on three intravenous drips by that time—dopamine and nitroprusside to try to manipulate the blood pressure in his body and lungs and priscoline, a powerful vasodilator that widened all the blood vessels in the body, which we hoped would do likewise for the narrowed ones in Harry's lungs. He had received so many boluses of various fluids to try to keep his heart full that he was starting to get puffy. And he was paralyzed with a drug called Pavulon, so he couldn't fight the ventilator. What else could we do? I wracked my tired brain, and then suddenly I remembered one of the PFC babies we'd had in San Francisco who had been in similarly dire straits. One of the attendings had tried Isuprel, a powerful cardiac stimulant, and somehow the baby had turned around. I remembered the baby's heart rate rising dangerously high, but she had turned pinker over several minutes. And I decided to try it on Harry.

Isuprel wasn't used very often in the NICU, so I got lots of questions about it from the staff. It took nearly an hour to get the order written, the drip prepared by the pharmacy, and the infusion started. Meanwhile, Harry was getting bradycardic—his heart rate dropping from 150 to 60—and we were about to start chest compressions when the Isuprel finally reached his bloodstream via his umbilical vein catheter. We could tell right away because his heart rate started to rise. At first, this was a relief because he'd become so bradycardic, but then we all became alarmed as it rose from 60 to 120 to 150, then 180, and finally 210. Unfortunately though, nothing else, except a slight increase in blood pressure, seemed to happen in response to the Isuprel. After the infusion had been going for about 20 minutes, one of the nurses got a blood gas reading from his umbilical artery catheter, and the results were virtually identical to the one obtained an hour earlier—his blood oxygen level was only 25. We were aiming for greater than 100. The blood test number matched the one displayed on the transcutaneous oxygen monitor attached to his chest wall. That number hadn't budged since the Isuprel had been started.

I left the baby's bedside and went back to the charting desk to call Sara, thinking that maybe I could talk her into traveling to Baltimore if I could convince her that it might be her only chance to see and perhaps hold her son before he died. As I dialed the hospital number, one of the nurses shouted at me to get back over to his bedside. I quickly dropped the phone and ran over, preparing to start a "Code" or full-scale resuscitation, which would likely prove futile. Instead, I was astonished to see that the number on Harry's transcutaneous oxygen monitor, which she was pointing to excitedly, was rising—rapidly. It read 50, then 55, then 60, then 80, then 100, and it kept rising. We all turned to look at Harry, and right there in front of our eyes, he began to turn pink, right down to his pudgy little toes. He'd opened up! It was a moment to cherish and remember, especially during those dark hours with other babies when nothing seemed to work.

Harry was still the sickest baby in the unit for the next day or two, but he never again turned blue and never came so close to death as he had in those hours before I'd started the Isuprel. I called Sara to give her the cautious good news before I finally left the hospital that evening. She had in fact signed herself out of the hospital AMA, and so I reached her at home. She sounded tired but very relieved that Harry was still hanging on and maybe, just maybe, had turned the corner.

A long, hot shower; a few bites of a delicious lemon-tuna pasta made by Erik; a glass of milk—and I was a goner. I slept like a rock that night, awakened only once by the resident in the NICU, who needed some advice about weaning the ventilator on one of our preemies. I asked her about Harry's oxygen level and she said she hadn't had to worry about him at all that night—his oxygen level had stayed well above 100 and in fact, she'd started cautiously weaning the amount of oxygen he was receiving.

A few days later, Harry was off all his drips and unbelievably, we were able to extubate him and take him off the ventilator.

Everyone commented on rounds that day what a cute baby he was, and "a great save" was mentioned several times. Now that he was really a "keeper," we spent more time on rounds discussing the difficult social issues that his mother's anorexia and agoraphobia presented. Although Sara had been calling the unit regularly to inquire about Harry, she hadn't given any indication that she was planning to visit, and most of us doubted whether she would have been able to come even if he'd died. So, what would happen to him after he was discharged from the hospital? Would his mother be able to take care of him when she had so many problems of her own to deal with? She wanted to breastfeed and was pumping her breasts. Was this safe, given her precarious nutritional state?

Later that day, I was returning to the NICU with my third cup of flavored coffee—amaretto this time—when I ran into George, one of the pediatric radiologists, who was wheeling out the portable ultrasound machine we used to scan the brains of our premature infants, who were so vulnerable to hemorrhaging.

"It looks really bad," he told me.

"Who are you talking about?" I asked.

"I just did that cranial ultrasound on that big kid in Room 1— the nurse called him Harry. He basically only has water in there where his cerebral cortex once was. The only thing he's got left is his brain stem. He's got hydranencephaly. His brain basically melted down some time ago. What made you order the study? You don't normally get head ultrasounds in term babies unless you suspect a neurological problem, and this kid looks like such a normal baby."

I was stunned. I knew that children who had hydranencephaly never did much more than they did as newborns. They could breathe, suck, swallow, cry, and even smile, because these are all primitive functions that are directed by the brain stem. But for anything more advanced, such as thinking or responding to your mother's voice, you needed your cerebral cortex. And if Harry had any cortex left, it was too small to be seen on the head ultrasound. If we had only known this a few days ago, we wouldn't have tried so hard to save his life. As we often said behind closed doors, his serious PFC condition could have been his "ticket out." Here I'd been, feeling so smug because I'd thought of starting Isuprel and that had turned out to be the magic bullet. But now, I felt sick inside. Maybe Harry hadn't been such a "great save" after all.

I still hadn't answered George's question, though. He'd wanted to know why I'd ordered the study in the first place, and my answer was—I hadn't ordered it. So who had? I walked back into the unit and found the four residents and my fellow, Joan, poring over a neonatal textbook together in their charting room—which was about the size of a small walk-in closet. The book was opened to the page on hydranencephaly. They all looked up at me when I appeared at the door.

"Have you heard about the cranial ultrasound on that PFC baby?" Joan asked me, although she must have seen by the look on my face that I had.

I nodded my head and then asked the sad little group who had ordered the study. Joan said that after rounds that morning, she had done a mini teaching session with the residents about the effects of severe maternal starvation or anorexia nervosa on the developing fetus. She'd read that sometimes—though rarely—severe fetal brain injuries or developmental disorders could occur, and so she'd decided to order a cranial ultrasound on Harry. Even though she, too, had been stunned by the results, she couldn't hide that proud glow I knew she must be feeling inside. She had been the one, not I, to suspect this zebra when she heard Harry's hoofbeats. And she'd been right. I'd been in her shoes when I was a fellow, and I knew exactly how she felt.

Although this was the first time I was upstaged by one of my trainees, it was by no means the last—and I believe that in addition

to wanting to do what's best for the babies in my care, it's what
drives me to keep myself up to date and continually on my toes
today, 20 years later. But back then, it was a very humbling experience for me. After all, I was the brand-new attending neonatologist
at Johns Hopkins Hospital. I was the head honcho, the top dog, the
big cheese. The buck stopped with me. Shouldn't *I* have been the
one to consider the impact of Sara's eating disorder on her baby's
developing brain?

I didn't really have much time to ponder that question. In the
NICU, we often followed that directive "don't just stand there,
do something" whenever something bad or unexpected happened.
Springing into action helped to take our minds off the difficult
emotional, moral, and ethical questions we struggled with. No one
yet dared to ask out loud what we were all asking ourselves inwardly.
Would we have tried so hard to save this baby's life if we'd known
that he essentially had no working brain left?

My little team of residents and my fellow now turned to me for
direction. What should we do now? Someone needed to let Harry's
mother know about this tragic turn of events and that difficult task
would be mine. After all, I'd kept in close contact with her during those first few days when Harry was critically ill—and I was
the attending. But first, I sat down with Joan for a few minutes to
discuss what she'd learned about hydranencephaly and to develop a
management plan for Harry. We decided that a pediatric neurology
consult would be helpful. Neonatologists generally saw the babies
only in the newborn period, either making the diagnosis or confirming what had been seen on a prenatal ultrasound. Neurologists
followed babies with hydranencephaly for the rest of their short
little lives.

Next, Joan and I took our team of residents over to Harry's
bedside to examine him together—looking for any outward signs
of the tragedy within his head—and to fill in his bedside nurse.

There were a lot of reasons why it was important that she know what was going on, but in my opinion, the most important was so that she could pick up the pieces after I'd spoken with Sara.

I grabbed the transilluminator, a small bright light that we used to highlight tiny veins or arteries so we could put catheters in them or to help diagnose a pneumothorax, by placing the light directly onto the baby's chest to see whether one side "lights up." When the group had assembled around Harry's crib, I positioned the sleeping, amazingly pink baby on his back and gently woke him. He started to cry, and I quickly found his "binky" and put it in his mouth. He immediately began sucking on it and opened his eyes. He looked just like every other normal full-term baby I'd ever seen. But then I positioned the transilluminator over the soft spot at the back of his head (every baby has two soft spots, not just the familiar one on the top of the head). I asked the bedside nurse to turn off the room lights for a minute, and then I turned on the transilluminator. Harry's little bald head lit up like a Christmas tree bulb. His skull wasn't that thick and there was no brain in the way to absorb the light—just fluid. I had read about this finding in textbooks, but I'd never actually seen it. It was a very sobering experience for us all.

After a few more teaching moments and conversation with Harry's nurse, I found Sara's home phone number and decided to call her from my office—away from all the noise and distractions of the NICU. I sat at my desk for a few minutes, collecting my thoughts and trying to prepare myself for the conversation ahead of me. We all dreaded being the bearer of bad news, and during my fellowship I saw numerous different attending styles. But it was Stephanie Berman, the social worker who had been my bad-news mentor back in San Francisco, whose style I had tried to emulate. What would she do? I wondered.

Sara answered on the second ring, and I reintroduced myself and then spent a few minutes bringing her up to date on Harry's amazing recovery from severe PFC. I also asked her how *she* was doing and she said it had been really hard not to be able to come and hold Harry, especially now that he was off the ventilator. She told me that her doctor had told her she couldn't travel, but we both knew that it was her agoraphobia that had kept her away from her baby when he needed her most.

My palms grew sweaty and I sat up straighter in my chair as I prepared to launch into the real reason I'd called.

"I'm afraid I have some bad news about Harry," I began. "We did an ultrasound of his head today because he'd been so sick, and we discovered that something very bad happened to his brain during your pregnancy. Basically, the thinking part of his brain—the cortex—is gone. All that he has left is the base of his brain—the brain stem. That's the part of our brain that directs the most basic things that newborn babies do, like breathing, crying, and even sucking on a pacifier. Harry looks really normal and can do all those basic things. But it's unlikely he'll ever be able to do more than that. I am so sorry that I have to give you such bad news."

There was a long silence after that; at least it seemed long to me. I am always tempted to interrupt that silence but I know that it's best to let it hang there, and to allow the parents to break it with their own questions. And Sara finally did.

"It's all my fault, isn't it?" she asked, for the second time. "If I'd been able to take better care of myself when I was pregnant, none of this would have happened to my poor baby."

I then launched into my usual response to that kind of query: We don't really understand why and how these things happen, but we know they can happen even when there are no problems at all during a pregnancy. But I knew that Sara probably didn't buy it, just as she hadn't bought it when I essentially said the same thing about his PFC. If we didn't know how this terrible thing could have happened to her baby's brain, then she would live with the

assumption that her own condition—her anorexia and whatever
went with that—must have caused it. And of course, from a medical perspective, I would agree with her.

I spent a few more minutes on the phone with Sara, explaining that I'd asked for a consultation from a pediatric neurologist
and that he would be able to help answer our questions about what
would likely happen to Harry over the next few weeks, months,
or possibly years. I asked her if there was someone she could turn
to—a friend, family member, clergy? I thought she might be crying as she murmured something about her mother being with her.
And then suddenly, the phone went dead. She'd hung up on me. I
waited a few minutes and redialed the number, but it was busy, and
it stayed busy when I tried again an hour later. She was either on
the phone with someone or had left the phone off the hook. I was
worried about what she might do, given her fragile mental health.
But there wasn't much that I could do other than fill in Linda, the
NICU social worker. She promised to keep trying Sara's phone and
also said she'd call the public health nurse who'd been assigned to
check on Sara when she'd left the hospital AMA.

The next day, the pediatric neurologist we'd consulted came to
see Harry and to review his head ultrasound. John was a nation-
ally renowned expert on pediatric epilepsy. I'd also learned that he
was quite outspoken and opinionated regarding controversial issues,
which were numerous in his field. He was a tall, imposing man
with a somewhat brusque manner. He confirmed the diagnosis of
hydranencephaly and spent some time with our team, discussing
the various theories about how and why this sometimes happened.
Still, fundamentally it was a mystery. We peppered him with questions about the "natural history" of these babies. What would happen to Harry? How long would he live? We were all surprised to
learn that although his neurodevelopmental prognosis was very
poor, there was actually some variability in how these kids turned

out. This was because you couldn't really tell from the ultrasound how much brain they had left, if any, and because you also couldn't predict the growth and development of other parts of their brain that could potentially take over some of the function of the missing cortex. He also told us that Harry would likely need a shunt at some point because the normal drainage system for cerebrospinal fluid was probably disrupted, allowing the fluid to build up in his head—enlarging it to the size of a watermelon, which would make it increasingly difficult to care for him.

When she'd called John to arrange the consult, Joan had briefly filled him in on Harry's initial critical illness and on Sara's mental health problems. I now directed the discussion toward the team's collective angst over what we'd done in saving Harry's life. Had we saved him for a life that would be worse than death? And would Sara's fragile condition now be made even worse, saddled with both her own guilt and the burden of caring for a severely disabled child? No one had heard from her since she'd hung up on me after I'd given her the terrible news.

I was taken aback when John turned to me and in a way, reprimanded me—for putting myself in her shoes and presuming to know how she would deal with Harry's condition and how it would affect her own life. And for regretting that we'd saved his life.

"You have no idea how this will turn out," he said. "I've followed families who were thrust in a situation that they never imagined they could deal with. And yet for some, not only do they rise to the occasion, their lives are actually made better for doing it."

"You can't mean that this could possibly have a good outcome for this family?" I asked him, feeling myself getting angry with him.

"I've seen amazing things happen, Chris," he said. "And you shouldn't just impose your own life view on this baby's mother. This could be the best thing that ever happened to her."

Incredulous, and admittedly somewhat affronted by his response, I then asked him, "Do you actually think we should have tried just as hard to save his life, even if we'd known he had hydranencephaly?"

"Well, let's just say that sometimes things happen for a reason," he replied, somewhat smugly in my opinion, "and even though you might know a lot about neonatology, you probably don't know all the reasons why babies like Harry get PFC or why whatever you did to save his life worked."

I felt very angry now, not so much because I disagreed with what he'd said (which I did), but because I felt somewhat put down in front of the residents and my fellow. I was an attending now and I felt a certain obligation to know it all when it came to my patients—or at least to act as if I did.

John was stat paged to the PICU for another neurology consult. Before he left, he told us that he would write a detailed consult note, give us some articles on hydranencephaly, and—perhaps most important—would be available to speak with Harry's mother, either by phone or in person, if she ever made it to Baltimore. And then he was gone, leaving me to try to lead the heated discussion that followed.

The next day, as work rounds were ending, I was paged overhead to the unit clerk's desk. A very thin young woman with a pale, drawn face had come into the unit on the arm of an older, somewhat obese woman. She had stopped at the front desk and asked for me. As soon as I saw her, I guessed that the young woman was Sara, and I was right. I extended my hand and she took it into both of hers. Her hands were so bony and her palms so sweaty. How could this poor thing absorb such a tragedy, let alone care for a baby with such a limited future?

But when she spoke, I sensed a different woman than the pathetic, fragile one I'd imagined from our phone conversations.

"I'm here to see my son, and to learn everything I need to know in order to take him home," she said, firmly and without even a quaver in her voice. "This is my mother," she said, indicating with a brief nod the woman to whose arm she was clinging. "She's been kind enough to bring me to the hospital, because I don't have my driver's license yet."

I was astonished. Here was a woman who, by all accounts, had not voluntarily left her home in three years—except to deliver her baby. Even though she was 19, she probably hadn't even taken driver's ed because she hadn't been able to get to the classes. I wondered whether she'd even finished high school. And yet here she was, determined to take care of her baby, a baby with essentially no brain—who would need a shunt and complete care for the rest of his life.

I never in a million years would have imagined the series of events that unfolded over the next several days. Sara spent most of each day on the unit, holding and rocking Harry and learning basic newborn baby care. Harry didn't require anything special at this point, so she was able to concentrate on things like burping, changing diapers, and giving him a bath. She and her mother stayed at a nearby hotel, eating their meals gratis at the hospital cafeteria—all of which must have been very difficult for her, given her terrible anxiety about public places. She met with John on several occasions and he must have answered all her questions, because she asked me very few. Once, she pointed to a baby on a ventilator with six drips hanging by her bedside and asked me whether that baby had what Harry had—that "PFC" thing, or whatever I'd called it. And I answered yes, this baby girl had the same problem as Harry, although she wasn't nearly as sick as he'd been.

Sara looked me in the eye then, and said, "Thank you so much for saving my baby's life. I love him more than anything."

I figured that she just didn't understand. After all, Harry looked so normal. She probably doesn't believe us, or the ultrasound, I thought to myself. It wouldn't be the first time a parent simply refused to believe what we told her, realizing the awful truth only when her baby didn't coo, roll over, sit up, or smile at her. But I was wrong. And John was right—and he made sure I knew it, too, making it a point to give me regular follow-up information after Harry had been discharged. Sara knew exactly what the future held for her and her baby, and she took him home anyway—with her mother's help and support. She and Harry, both in their own way, began a lifetime of intensive therapy. Sara entered an inpatient treatment program for people with eating disorders, and in six weeks she learned to deal with both that and her agoraphobia. She was driven by a single mission—her son needed her, and she wanted to be there, and to be healthy, for him. Harry had numerous visits to the pediatric neurology clinic at Hopkins where John oversaw his shunt placement, which was needed as his head growth rapidly accelerated, and various physical therapy sessions designed to maximize his very limited potential.

About a year after Harry had been discharged home, I was sitting in my office, working on a new research grant, when there was a knock at my door. When I opened it, there was Sara and there sat Harry in a stroller. I gazed at him for a moment. Despite the shunt, his head was noticeably larger than normal. His eyes didn't hold my gaze but rather wandered, seemingly aimlessly, around the room. And he was making funny smacking noises with his lips. Possible seizures, I thought.

Sara came up to me and hugged me, for a long time.

"We just came from one of our neurology clinic visits," she said, "and I told Dr. John that we just had to stop by and thank Dr. Chris for giving us one of the best years of our lives."

I know I must have blushed, because I do that when I'm embarrassed. And I was embarrassed not by her gratitude—we all cherished miraculous outcomes and grateful parents—but because I had never guessed that what I had done would ever be worthy of someone's gratitude. I also knew, in my heart, that if I'd known that Harry had hydranencephaly, I would have "let him go" when that time came—and definitely not started Isuprel. I would have deprived her of this time and, indeed, of this transforming experience in her life.

Sara then proceeded to tell me all the wonderful things that Harry had accomplished in his first year of life. He smiled at her, and apparently only at her; he reached for a certain toy that he loved; and he never cried. He was such a good, happy baby, and she loved him more than anything. She told me she knew she wouldn't have him for long but would love every single minute she had with him. And oh, by the way, her own problems (did I remember those? she asked) were all history now. She'd known that in order to really be Harry's mother, she'd have to fix her own life. She'd decided to become a nurse—when she had time to go to school, that is. We both knew what she meant. After Harry had died.

A couple of months after that visit to my office, John stopped by to tell me that Harry had died at home, peacefully, in his mother's arms. We had a brief conversation then about his initial consultation. I told him how angry I'd been at his opinions about the quality of Harry's life, especially the impact that Harry might have on Sara's life. And I admitted that he'd been right and I'd been wrong.

I sent Sara a sympathy card and she wrote back to me, thanking me again for all I'd done for Harry and telling me that she'd been accepted into nursing school and would start classes in the fall. Harry, in his short life and in his death, had given Sara her life back. I pondered, for a long time, the limitations of my knowledge. I had begun to realize, not for the first time, and certainly not for the last, that being a good neonatologist involved lifelong learning—and not just from books or lectures. My training didn't stop at the end of my fellowship or when I became "board-certified." I had so much to learn from more experienced clinicians like John, from my trainees, and of course from the families and the babies I cared for. I vowed to keep learning, for the rest of my career, how to truly "practice" the art of medicine.

CHAPTER 15

Baby X

IT WAS A COLD gray day in late January. I sat alone on a folding chair, sequestered in a small room at the back of the main courtroom of the Baltimore City Courthouse. I was waiting to be called as an expert witness to testify in a manslaughter case. As I sat there, I went over the relevant facts of the case and my testimony, which I'd rehearsed with the prosecutor the day before. The main question was this: Was the baby born alive or not? The defendant's fate rested on whether or not I could convince the jury that she had been born alive, and therefore, that he'd killed her.

She was born on a warm, sultry Baltimore evening the previous June. I was the attending in the NICU and after almost two years at Hopkins, I was thoroughly broken in. The NICU was relatively quiet and my work was done, so I left at about five o'clock. with a singular mission on my mind. Erik and I had decided we were ready to start a family. We'd been married for two years, preceded by three years of stormy dating and several broken engagements. I was 34 years old and my biologic clock was ticking insistently. That night, the stars were aligned for conception, or at least that's what the little urine test strip I'd used that morning had predicted.

Afterward, Erik put together a simple dinner—pork chops and rice—while I sat on a bar stool by the window in our little kitchen, which I loved. I wished that I could have a glass of wine, but I never, ever did when I was on call. What if I made a mistake? Doctors do make mistakes, but if I'd had even a few sips of wine, I would have always wondered if somehow that had impaired my judgment.

Just as we were sitting down to dinner, the phone rang. I sighed and got up to answer it, knowing it was probably someone at the hospital. And it was in fact Cheryl, one of the nurses in the NICU. She told me that the residents and the rest of the NICU's resuscitation team had been paged stat to the ER for an emergency cesarean section. She had no idea what was going on, but the senior resident had shouted to her to "call Chris" as he ran through the swinging doors, tackle box in hand. It must be a trauma case, I told Cheryl, thinking about the worst-case scenario—a bad auto accident in which the pregnant driver took a major hit to her abdomen with the steering wheel. I said I'd be there in 20 minutes.

I hung up the phone, threw on some clothes, kissed Erik good-bye, and flew out the door. I was glad that it was summer, and therefore still light out. I drove past dilapidated row houses with clusters of mostly women and children gathered on the stoops; past corner liquor stores with iron bars covering the windows and door, and always a few men standing or stumbling around; and past several police cars parked at odd angles in front of a store or row house. Baltimore had one of the highest homicide rates in the nation at that time, with more than 300 murders in the city in one year—the victims being mostly young black men. Once, in the middle of the night, I paused at a red light—a Baltimore police officer once advised me to treat stop lights like stopsigns when driving through the city in the middle of the night—and saw an officer on one knee beside his cruiser with his gun drawn. I ducked my head and ran the light. But that June night, East

Baltimore looked almost bucolic, and I made it to the hospital in record time.

I ran through the parking garage and then along one of the hospital's long corridors toward the emergency room, a place I had visited only once during my two years at Hopkins, and then only to tend to a baby who just couldn't wait for her mother to make it to the Labor and Delivery unit. Those babies were usually kicking and screaming by the time our team got down there. This scenario was to be completely different.

There must have been 50 people squeezed into the main trauma room, which mostly dealt with gunshot victims. The big auto accidents usually went to the Maryland Shock Trauma unit, although we occasionally got those victims, too, especially if the accident occurred in East Baltimore. There were at least a dozen police officers along with numerous men and women in scrubs — ER docs, nurses, surgeons, and residents. I recognized none of them. I caught a glimpse of the woman who I assumed was the victim, being worked on in the center of the room by a team of people in surgical garb. They didn't look particularly frantic, and that's because, as I was to learn later, she had already been pronounced dead.

"Where's the baby?" I called out to the assembled crowd.

Someone pointed in the direction of another room down the corridor and there I found my team, along with a few additional people I didn't recognize. I identified myself as the attending neonatologist and it was as though the waters parted as I moved toward the baby's wet, bloody head and reached for a stethoscope. She had been intubated and was now being hand-bagged. She wasn't yet attached to a pulse oximeter, but I could tell that she was more or less pink. I could also see that someone had placed an intraosseous line — a big needle in the bone on her lower leg — presumably to give fluid and drugs. I wondered why no one had thought to put in an umbilical vessel catheter.

"How old is she and what's been done so far?" I asked Sam, the senior resident, who looked surprisingly calm. Shelly, his intern, on the other hand, looked like a deer in the headlights.

"Fifteen minutes," he replied. "Once they made the decision to deliver the baby, they had her out in less than five minutes. Her Apgar at one minute was zero. No heart rate. Nothing."

It was that tiny piece of her short life story that was to form the keystone of the public defender's case. A baby with an Apgar score of zero was a dead baby. If there really was no heart rate, then the heart must have stopped. You could perhaps bring it back, as they might have done in this case, but if the heart really wasn't beating at birth, the baby was born dead. One catch, though: The tools that we use, even now, to detect a newborn baby's heart rate are pretty crude—at least compared with the sophisticated monitoring equipment we use in the NICU. And in a delivery situation like this—an emergency C-section in an adult ER, away from our special infant resuscitation setups—our tools were even cruder. Someone likely listened to her chest with a stethoscope (which could have been turned the wrong way in the excitement) and simultaneously, someone had probably felt for a pulsation in her umbilical cord. When a baby had a very low blood pressure, as was likely the case here, you often couldn't feel or hear the heart rate, even when it was there.

Sam had few details about what had happened to the mother that had led to the emergency delivery of her baby. He'd heard something about her being shot. He filled me in briefly on the resuscitation, explaining that as the NICU team was drying and stimulating the baby, suctioning out her mouth and nose and applying bag-and-mask ventilation, all the while trying to detect a heartbeat, an anesthesiologist had pushed him out of the way and intubated the baby. I knew how Sam must have felt. That was *his* job and one that by now, in his third year of residency, he felt quite competent doing. I reminded him that that's what anesthesiologists do best—they intubate and they pass gas.

Everyone in the room laughed, even the anesthesiologist who'd intubated the baby. He had backed away when I'd come in and was now standing by the door. Sam then went on to explain that once he'd realized there was no detectable heart rate, he'd ordered a dose of epinephrine to be put down the tube while a nurse performed cardiopulmonary resuscitation. Someone had put in the intraosseous line—he wasn't sure who had done that—and Sam had then ordered a bolus of fluid and another dose of epi to be given through that line. By the time all that had been done—Sam estimated that 10 minutes had elapsed—CPR was halted for a moment and as he'd listened over the baby's chest, he'd detected a heartbeat. She'd been resuscitated, brought back to life. And I'd walked in about five minutes later.

"Great job, Sam," I said, giving him a big pat on the back. I knew that he, like every pediatric resident I'd ever known, needed that positive feedback. "My guess is, though, since her heart rate 'came back' relatively quickly, that she must have had a heart rate to begin with. You just couldn't pick it up because she was so hypotensive. If her heart had really, truly stopped beating, it would have taken a lot more to jump-start it back up."

I then took a closer look at the baby. She was big—I estimated at least eight pounds. She was very pale but had an impressive head of curly black hair. I didn't realize during that brief exam that she was black, although that's not so unusual. Sometimes a black baby's skin color doesn't come in for several days or even weeks after birth. She was completely motionless—not even taking an occasional breath or gasp—and when I briefly picked up her arm and let it go, it just flopped back down onto the bed. She had no muscle tone. I listened over her chest with the stethoscope and heard air from the bag moving easily in and out of her lungs, and saw her chest rising and falling with each breath. I also heard a faint heartbeat, but when I felt her neck and groin for a pulse, I couldn't feel a thing. Her blood pressure must be very low, I thought. And she wasn't as pink as she should have been, given that she was being bagged with 100 percent oxygen.

"She needs more fluid," I pronounced to the little group. "Now."

A nurse drew up some saline solution into a large syringe and prepared to push it into the intraosseous line the baby had in her leg.

"Not there," I said. The site already looked swollen and red. Who knew whether the tip of the needle was in the right place, or if she'd even received the medications and fluid they'd put in there earlier?

"Let's slip in an umbilical catheter, like we usually do," I told Sam.

He nodded and got a catheter out of the tackle box they'd brought down from the NICU. He quickly prepared the baby's umbilical cord, which had a big surgical clamp hanging onto it, with some antiseptic solution. He then put a cord tie around the base of the cord, tied it snugly, and made a clean cut across the cord with a knife. There are no nerves in the umbilical cord, so cutting the cord doesn't hurt. Three blood vessels stood out on the baby's umbilical stump, like little soldiers. The two smaller ones were the arteries and the bigger, thin-walled one was the vein. That's the one Sam put the catheter into, and as soon as he was able to draw some blood back with a syringe, he took the saline-filled syringe from the nurse and proceeded to slowly infuse the large amount of fluid into the baby. I instructed Sam to place a smaller catheter into one of the umbilical arteries, as long as he was right there. I put on a pair of sterile gloves and prepared that catheter for him while he finished pushing the saline in. He then took less than a minute to place that umbilical artery catheter, which was always more difficult than the wider-mouthed vein. I felt an inner glow of pride, just as I was to feel later on when one of my children accomplished some milestone.

The baby's response to that saline fluid push was just like that of a plant receiving water. We watched as she almost immediately pinked up. Now we could easily palpate her pulses. She must have lost a fair amount of blood, probably during the delivery or as part of whatever had happened to her poor mother. Or perhaps her stressed, overworked little heart just needed to be filled up a bit more. We would teach the residents that even when the newborn heart is pumping as hard and fast as it can, the cardiac output won't improve unless "the tank is full." We'd filled this little girl's tank, and she looked much better for it.

Sadly, though, this successful heart and lung resuscitation didn't seem to have worked as well on her brain. She remained motionless except for sudden sharp intakes of breath that we called agonal gasps. While at first glance these breaths seemed like a hopeful sign that she was coming around, I suspected that instead, they heralded the onset of those terrible signs of brain damage that we saw in severely asphyxiated babies. Soon, I predicted to the NICU team gathered there, she would start having generalized clonus, meaning that her entire body would shake and shudder as though she were having continual seizures. Clonus was the worst neurological sign and always reminded me of Linda, the 14-year-old asthmatic girl who had died a brain death during one of my PICU rotations as a resident. It was also very difficult to manage, because the shaking didn't respond to the typical antiseizure medications we used. And it was terribly difficult for family members and staff to watch.

As I mused about this little girl's immediate future in my NICU, I realized that now would be a good time to find out more about what had happened to her mother, before the crowds in the ER dispersed. Even though all the people gathered there, attending to the victim, would be thinking that they'd never forget what happened, the truth was that soon, the details would indeed be lost, replaced by other equally or sometimes more terrifying scenarios. The baby had stabilized enough to be transported to the NICU, and I knew the team could handle the move without me.

I returned to the trauma room, where I saw the baby's mother lying motionless, just like her daughter, in the center of the room—now covered with a bloody white sheet. I could see one of her hands, extending beyond the edge of the sheet, dangling lifelessly over the edge of the table she lay on. She had long, beautifully manicured red fingernails, one of which looked as though it had recently broken.

I recognized one of the hospital obstetricians. He was talking to one of the police officers and when he'd finished, I asked him if he knew what had happened.

"It doesn't get much worse than this, Chris," he said. "This woman was nine months pregnant and she was shot, skewered really, with an arrow fired from one of those hunting bow-and-arrow weapons. It went in one side of her abdomen and out the other. It missed the baby but tore through some big blood vessels. She basically bled to death before she even got to the ER. When the ER team realized that she wasn't going to make it, they decided to open her up and just get the baby out, hoping that at least something could be done to save the child. I was stat paged just as they were getting ready to make the incision in her uterus. They were pushing huge amounts of blood into her and pumping on her chest, just trying to maintain a blood pressure for the baby's sake. I've never seen so much blood coming from anyone's abdomen, though. Basically, everything they were pushing in was just coming back out through those big vessel tears."

"Who would do such a thing?" I asked, stunned at this unfathomable display of Baltimore's homicidal violence. The next morning, everyone would read in the *Baltimore Sun* that the woman was an innocent bystander, caught in the crossfire of a drug deal gone bad, just as she was preparing to cross the street in her neighborhood. The shooter apparently had not received what he felt was coming to him and as his "customer" took off down the sidewalk, he disappeared into his row house and picked up the hunting bow and arrow. He aimed at the fleeing man, later claiming that he'd called out to the obviously pregnant woman in his line of fire to get out of the way. One witness said she'd looked startled, uncertain of what to do, and then he suddenly let his fatal arrow fly.

The baby "lived" for another three days, if you could call generalized clonus, seizures, and periodic agonal gasping living. An electroencephalogram, or brain wave study, was ordered by the neurologist I'd consulted and this was basically "flat line" except for occasional spikes of seizurelike electrical activity—a very ominous pattern that was termed "burst suppression." Determination of brain death in newborns is not as straightforward as it is in older children or adults. That's because normal newborn neurological functions are controlled primarily by the brain stem, which develops first and sits at the base of the brain, which is a relatively protected area. However, in this case, even the baby's brain stem had not been protected. She wasn't breathing and had difficulty regulating her own body temperature. Everyone agreed that by virtually any criteria that could be applied, her brain had taken a terrible, irreversible hit, most likely as a result of her lifeline—the placenta—being essentially cut off as her mother's lifeblood drained from her.

Several relatives showed up to visit the baby. Most stood quietly by her bedside, sometimes stroking her beautiful curly head of hair or holding her little hand in theirs. They would look alarmed and sad when she suddenly shook or quivered. Someone stuck two little pink bows over each of her temples. And several stuffed animals appeared at the head of her bed. Lots of tears were shed.

A tall, slender man had identified himself as the baby's father and I spent some time talking with him about her, and as I got to know him a bit better, about the baby's mother. She'd led a hard life, and so had he—or at least that was my take on his somewhat rambling comments—but they were both looking forward to the birth of this baby. She'd never finished high school, but she'd recently been talking about enrolling in night classes so that she could get her high school equivalency diploma. She was tired of the life she'd been living and now that she was going to be a mother, she wanted a change. He said he had felt the same way, but now, what reason did he have to change his way of life?

I asked him whether they'd already picked out a name for the baby and he said that no, they just couldn't agree. If it was a girl, she'd favored names like Latoya or Laquisha but he'd wanted something entirely different, something like Eleanor or Elizabeth. None of the relatives had been able to agree on a name either, and he just couldn't bring himself to simply give her a name when they hadn't agreed on one.

So, she died without a name in the arms of her father, surrounded by family members. No one had to make a decision to "pull the plug"; she did that herself. Her heart had taken as big a hit as her brain, as it turned out, and it never pumped well during her short life. On the afternoon of her third day of life, her heart rate suddenly slowed down and her blood pressure dropped. It was time to say good-bye, and luckily, everyone was gathered nearby. At 3:58 P.M., recorded officially on the medical record, she was pronounced dead—the defense attorney would claim that it was her second death because she'd been born dead. All I kept thinking was that now she was together again with her mother, from whom she'd been so abruptly and tragically separated.

Now, as I sat in the cold, damp little room at the back of the Baltimore City Courthouse, I recalled that bedside scene, and the father's sad eyes. And I felt a wave of anger pass through me at the thought of the shooter's apparently random, senseless act of violence, which had robbed that man of his girlfriend and baby daughter—and perhaps the beginning of a new life for all of them.

The bailiff knocked and then opened the door to my little waiting room, announcing that it was my turn to take the witness stand. I got up slowly, feeling butterflies in my stomach and chest. It was actually the second time I'd been in a courtroom (I'd contested a traffic ticket when I was a medical student), but this was completely different. My testimony could make the difference in whether the shooter would be convicted of manslaughter in the death of the baby. He'd already been convicted of murder in the death of her mother. But Maryland state law at that time stated that even if you killed a pregnant woman and as a consequence, her fetus, you couldn't be convicted separately of killing the fetus unless the baby was born alive and then died because of what you'd done to the mother. I needed to convince the jury therefore that the baby had been live-born—something that I was absolutely convinced was true.

The bailiff held open one of the heavy wooden double doors at the back of the courtroom for me and I walked in, heading toward the witness stand. Just like in the movies, the heads of several of those seated in the gallery—including the shooter, sitting next to the public defender in the front row—turned toward me. A few gasps went up from that crowd as I lumbered down the aisle, my hands clasped together under my huge, protruding abdomen. I was nine months pregnant.

This fact hadn't been revealed to the defense team and the visual effect was dramatic. Here I was, the baby's doctor, at just about the same stage of pregnancy as that poor mother was when she was impaled by that arrow.

After I was sworn in and took my seat on the witness stand, I was asked to go through my credentials, starting with medical school. As I was talking, I glanced over at the defendant, whom I recognized from newspaper clippings and from the handcuffs on his wrists. He stared right back at me, and I felt a cold shiver run up and down my back. This was not a good man.

The prosecutor asked me some specific questions about the baby's resuscitation, including her one-minute Apgar score of zero. Since I hadn't been there at the very beginning, I simply expressed my opinion about why I thought she'd actually had a heart rate at birth, based upon my findings when I'd arrived. He then asked me whether there was anything else about the baby that had convinced me that she wasn't born dead, and I said yes, there was. I explained that I had considered the burst suppression pattern on her EEG and her unremitting seizures and generalized clonus as signs that her brain was alive. While these findings also showed that her brain had been terribly, irreversibly, and yes, even fatally damaged, they also indicated to me that part of her brain was alive—and therefore must have been born alive. Not *functionally* alive, which was how we determined brain death, but at least electrically alive. How else could her brain fire off those electrical discharges, those abnormal spikes?

My testimony was more my opinion than medical or scientific fact, but coupled with my credentials, and some supportive testimony from one of the ER doctors, who was convinced he'd heard a fetal heartbeat when he'd put a stethoscope over her bloody abdomen, it was persuasive enough to convict the killer of manslaughter in the baby's death. This added another seven years to his 25-year sentence for her mother's murder. And maybe, just maybe, that manslaughter conviction would be enough to stop someone else from killing another pregnant woman.

Three weeks later, Erik and I welcomed our firstborn child into our world—a beautiful, red-haired, long-legged baby girl who was nameless for two days because we just couldn't agree on what name suited her best, now that we could actually see her and touch her. She cried a lot in those first few weeks and that cry pierced my soul more deeply than anything else I had ever experienced. One night, she just wouldn't stop crying. We fed her, changed her, held her, sang to her, read to her—Erik, Kipling's poetry, and me *Goodnight Moon*—fed her again, and walked and bounced her around the apartment. Nothing seemed to help. Finally, at about 3 A.M., Erik and I put her in her crib with a pacifier held against her mouth with a blanket so it would stay put. But it must have popped out when she wound up for another good cry because as soon as we lay down exhausted in our bed, we heard that now familiar wail. Exasperated, Erik exclaimed, "You're a doctor. What's wrong with her? Why won't she stop crying? Why can't you do something?" Tears rolled down my cheeks and I started sobbing. Here I was, after four years of medical school, three years of pediatric residency, and three years of neonatology fellowship training and I didn't know what to do with my own neonate.

And then suddenly, I knew just where to turn. Just like in the NICU, I needed an authoritative book where I could search for the answers to Erik's and my desperate questions. When she learned we were expecting, Erik's sister Karen had given us an autographed hardcover 40th-anniversary edition of *Dr. Spock's Baby and Child Care*. Dr. Spock would know what to do. As our beloved daughter continued to wail in her crib, Erik and I huddled together in bed and began reading aloud the chapter entitled "Crying in the Early Weeks." When we came to the sentence that ended with "the important thing to remember is that these most common types of crying in the early weeks are temporary and are not a sign of anything serious," our baby suddenly stopped crying. We tiptoed in and watched her peacefully, blissfully sleeping, and we experienced the most overwhelming sense of relief.

And so I began the next phase of my career as a neonatologist. For even after all my training and now with three years under my belt as an attending neonatologist at Johns Hopkins Hospital, becoming a parent made me see things from a completely different perspective. And I realized I had so much more to learn.

Mitchell and Michael

FAST-FORWARD TO late August 2002. I was the attending neonatologist in the NICU at the University of Washington Medical Center in Seattle and I was nearing the end of a typical day—leading morning rounds with the residents and staff; examining babies and dictating progress notes; admitting one baby to the unit; holding a "care conference" with a family whose very premature baby had survived numerous crises and now needed a surgical procedure; and doing a prenatal consultation for a couple expecting a baby with several birth defects. As I passed by the front desk of the unit on my way home, the unit clerk stopped me.

"They need another prenatal consult on Labor and Delivery, Chris," she said as she handed me the phone message. "They don't think she'll deliver tonight, so maybe you could put it off till tomorrow."

I glanced at the slip of paper, which in addition to the mother's last name—Chessup—and her room number—8—had the words "28-week-twins" written on it. Putting my things down, I sighed. "You never know with twins," I told her. "They can be so unpredictable."

Before I walked into a room to do a prenatal consult, I always looked through the patient's chart and checked with the obstetrical staff first to find out what was going on. The charting room was the chief gathering place on the Labor and Delivery unit and as I walked in, it was the usual controlled chaos. Attending obstetricians, fellows, residents, and nursing staff all milled about beneath a large whiteboard on which patient names, gestation, stage of labor, and any other relevant bits of information were displayed. Sometimes it amazed me how easily the enormous complexities of a woman's identity and her pregnancy could be reduced to so few words scrawled on a whiteboard.

I searched for the name Chessup and found it next to Room 8 along with the information I already knew—28-week twins—but in addition, someone had scrawled the following: A-IUGR, ROM 19WKS. This meant that Twin A hadn't been growing well (intrauterine growth restricted) and worse, the amniotic sac around that twin had apparently ruptured (rupture of membranes) nine weeks ago, at only 19 weeks' gestation. This did not bode well for Twin A. For reasons that are poorly understood, fetuses need lots of amniotic fluid around them in order for their lungs to grow and develop properly. If Twin A's amniotic fluid had continued to leak out, then that twin's lungs would not only be premature but in addition, lung growth and development would likely be arrested at a very primitive stage. If that was the case, the prognosis for survival was poor.

I found the Chessups' attending obstetrician and asked him how much the twins' parents had been told about this additional complication.

"When her membranes ruptured at 19 weeks," he explained, "I basically told them that if the amniotic fluid leak didn't seal over, allowing the fluid to reaccumulate, then that twin could be in trouble."

"So what's happened?" I asked.

"She's continued to leak fluid for these past nine weeks. Every ultrasound has shown very little fluid around Twin A," he answered. "Doesn't look good," he added, "and the Chessups know that."

I thanked him for the information and for keeping the family so well informed. Sometimes it seemed as though the obstetricians left the bad news for us to break and prospective parents were understandably shocked, thinking they'd gotten through the worst and now everything was going to be all right.

I located Diane Chessup's medical chart amid the dozen or so that were scattered on the counters and table of the small charting room and quickly glanced through it. I found that the Chessups were a couple whose twin pregnancy, their first, had likely come as a complete surprise because it wasn't the result of in vitro fertilization, or IVF as it is popularly known. Both the Chessups had doctoral degrees and worked in the nearby university district. I jotted down a few relevant medical details about the pregnancy and then headed off to Room 8.

Taking a deep breath, I knocked on the door and heard two voices murmur in response, which I took to mean that it was okay for me to come in.

It was a typical labor and delivery room. The pregnant woman—who was usually perfectly healthy—had suddenly assumed the role of patient, lying resignedly on a hospital bed, her long hair spread out behind her and a thick-wide belt fastened around her exposed abdomen. The belt's cables were connected to a monitor that beeped out two sets of heartbeats, one for each twin. The father sat in a chair beside the bed, holding his wife's hand. They both looked at me expectantly as I walked into the room.

I introduced myself, explaining that I was a neonatologist, a pediatrician who specialized in the care of newborn babies. Then, before I launched into my typical talk about preemies, I asked them to tell me what they knew so far about their pregnancy. Over the years, I had found that this approach works better than me simply talking *at* people. For one thing, it got the parents talking, which allowed me to gauge the depth of their understanding and their chief concerns.

Alan, the prospective father, spoke first. "We've heard that most babies born at 28 weeks' gestation survive, which we think is pretty amazing," he began. "But we've also heard that they can have some complications which can lead to brain damage—and that really scares us." He looked at his wife, Diane. "Is there anything else?" he asked her.

Diane started to speak, and then paused as though she needed to collect herself. "Well, our OB has been worried about the fluid around Mitchell—that's Twin A. Did you know that I've been leaking fluid since 19 weeks?" she asked.

"Yes, I've heard about that," I told them, "and it really worries me, too." I began going through an explanation of why Mitchell's lung problems could be so much more severe than his twin's, but Alan cut me off.

"We understand that he may not make it," he said somewhat bluntly, "but we want everything done for him. If it looks hopeless, we want to know. We don't want him to suffer just because we want him so badly," he said, with a quick catch in his throat and a sidelong glance at Diane.

I'm continually amazed by the inner strength and resolve of so many parents who are suddenly thrust into such terrible situations, and the Chessups were no exception. They'd had some time to come to grips with the guarded prognosis for their firstborn and they'd already begun preparing themselves for the worst, while still hoping desperately for the best.

"Let's talk first about the basics of having premature babies," I suggested and when I saw them both nod, I plunged into my standard preemie talk, covering issues that both twins would face just because they would likely be born at 28 weeks' gestation, a full 12 weeks before their official due date. They knew that both their twins were boys—likely identical—and that generally speaking, boys had a harder time of it than girls, which in this case could be a double whammy for Mitchell, Twin A.

When I'd finished, I asked Alan and Diane if they had any questions and they both shook their heads. They'd already read a lot about premature babies, given that they were expecting twins. Later, when I'd gotten to know them quite well as NICU parents, I told them how impressed I'd been that they'd already taken and passed "Preemie 101."

I spent the remainder of my prenatal consult time with them talking about Mitchell, following up on Alan's earlier statement that they wanted "everything done" but didn't want him to suffer if it was hopeless. I explained that if Mitchell's lungs required very high pressures in order to ventilate them, the lungs were likely to rupture—the medical term for that was pneumothorax. If that happened, I told them, it would be unlikely that anything we could do to relieve the problem would change his poor outcome. In fact, putting in a chest tube would just cause him a lot more pain and discomfort. A pneumothorax would be the baby's way of sending us a signal that further aggressive therapy would be futile. It would be time to say good-bye.

Alan and Diane both looked down and then at each other. They seemed to understand what I was saying. The room was silent for a moment, save for the beeping of the fetal monitor.

We exchanged a few more words, and then I shook Alan's hand and grasped Diane's in both of mine. I assured them that I would keep them informed every step of the way and that taking care of their twins would be a team process—and they, the parents, were vital members of that team. As I started to walk toward the door,

Diane suddenly called out, "Dr. Gleason, do you think he has a chance?"

I paused. "If I thought the situation was hopeless," I replied slowly, "then I would not recommend doing anything, right from the very beginning. But there's so much we don't know about the mechanics of fetal lung development, including the specifics of why, and how much, amniotic fluid is needed. And that gives me hope that maybe there was enough for Mitchell. So yes, I think he has a chance. Perhaps not a very good chance, but a chance nonetheless."

Diane looked at me gratefully while Alan looked away. I guessed that he must be thinking that I was falsely raising her hopes. I wondered that, too. I tried to think of other babies I had cared for who had ruptured membranes so early in gestation, without sealing the leak. Had any of them survived? I couldn't think of one.

I stopped in the L & D charting room on my way out and jotted down a note summarizing my discussion with the Chessups. No one thought she would deliver that night; she had only some vague contractions and had been feeling some back pressure. Still, it was always important for the gist of my conversation with the parents to be immediately available to any staff who needed to know. I made it clear that they wanted everything done for their twins—up to a point. If the situation became hopeless for Twin A, they didn't want to prolong his suffering.

I made it home in time for dinner, which was a rarity when I was attending. My three daughters were filled with stories about the highs and lows of their school days, and Erik and I tried to give each one equal time. Dinner was delicious—a lemon-tuna pasta, one of my favorites among Erik's creations. I was just starting to fill the dishwasher—Erik and I had a kind of "prenup" in which we'd agreed that whoever cooked dinner would not have to clean up—when the phone rang. It was Kay, the unit clerk in the NICU.

"They need you in L & D right away," she told me.

"Do you know who's delivering?" I asked her.

"No idea," she told me. "The residents and nurses just ran over there and said to call Chris."

I grabbed my purse and ID card and made sure I had a pair of reading glasses in my pocket, in case I needed to be the one to put the endotracheal tube into the baby's trachea—necessary if we needed to help the baby breathe or to give liquid surfactant. When I'd turned 40, I'd suddenly realized that I couldn't see up close as well as I had before. Reading glasses had become an occupational necessity, and I had a pair near every delivery room and unit where I worked.

I stopped in the unit for just a second to drop off my purse and to grab a jumpsuit to put over my street clothes. Unlike the residents, fellows, and obstetricians, I never wore hospital scrubs anymore. It seemed to me that nice professional clothes under a crisp white coat imparted a certain air of confidence and perhaps a stronger sense, among the often distraught parents I dealt with, that I knew what I was doing. But it wouldn't do to wear street clothes in a clean delivery room, particularly if an operative delivery (C-section) was needed. So these hospital jumpsuits were always at the ready for me and my colleagues who needed to suit up in a hurry.

I ran over to the ISR. Every unit I've ever worked in has had its own name for the room or area near the delivery room where high-risk newborns are taken to be resuscitated or stabilized. ISR stood for the Infant Stabilization Room. Other monikers included "Crisis Room," "Resuss Room," and one of my favorites, "The Chute," so named because high-risk babies could be passed directly from the delivery room through a hole in the wall into the waiting arms of the resuscitation team.

The ISR was a small room with two swinging doors, one of which connected it directly to the main delivery/operating room and the other to a large central area where all the scrub sinks were located. The room was kept at 85 degrees so we could keep even the smallest preemies warm while we worked on them. There were two resuscitation tables positioned opposite one another, each with its own set of resuscitation equipment and monitors. A baby would be carried in on a towel or blanket directly from the delivery room, usually by one of the residents, and placed on his or her back with feet pointing toward the wall and the head and chest, where most of the resuscitation action took place, readily accessible to the team. When twins were being resuscitated, they were literally head to head, so there was always a lot of "excuse me" and "sorry about that" as the two teams often collided in that small space, particularly those members assigned to secure each baby's airway or breathing tube.

I pushed through the swinging door while still tying on my face mask and quickly surveyed the scene. Two teams were assembled, one at each of the two tables. Must be twins, I thought, and then I realized I'd arrived after the fact. One baby was already "out" and was being worked on by most of the resuscitation team. The room seemed hotter than usual, and there were beads of sweat on most of the foreheads.

"What's the story?" I asked the team waiting by the empty resuscitation table, as I moved over to the table where the other team was working on one twin.

"It's 28-week twins," someone said. "And one of them's been ruptured since 19 weeks." Oh no, I thought. It must be the Chessups.

"What happened?" I asked.

Someone said something about a cord prolapse on Twin A. If that had happened—his umbilical cord coming out ahead of him, potentially cutting off his blood supply—it would have prompted an emergency cesarean section. I looked down at the baby being resuscitated on the warming table and was surprised to see that he was pink and breathing on his own. I could even hear a few kittenlike cries as the team gently stimulated him, incredible for a baby who'd had so little amniotic fluid for such a long time *and* a prolapsed cord. If these were the Chessup twins, then this had to be Michael, Twin B, extracted first from the womb because he must have been closer to the "top" during the rapid-fire C-section.

Just then the swinging door from the delivery room flew open, and in came the second twin in the arms of the intern. This must be Mitchell, I thought, and I braced myself for the worst.

The intern laid her little bundle down on the empty resuscitation table, blankets and all. She announced breathlessly, to no one in particular, "The OBs said that this is the bad one. No amniotic fluid and they lost the heart rate a few minutes before delivery."

The team assigned to this twin quickly swung into action. Normally this meant that the senior resident directed the resuscitation, but since the only other physician there was a brand-new intern, I took the lead. Secretly I was relieved, because I knew that this baby would need someone with a lot of experience, not just in various procedures but in making difficult decisions—such as when to say that enough is enough.

The nurse quickly dried off the baby and began gently stimulating him while the respiratory therapist attached an electrode to his foot, which connected him to the pulse oximeter, a monitor that hung over the foot of the table and displayed, audibly and visibly, the baby's heart rate and level of oxygenation. At the same time, seeing that the baby was making no effort to breathe, and in fact wasn't moving at all, I used a suction catheter to clear his mouth and nose of secretions and then applied a small mask to his face, which was connected to a breathing bag. I began trying to inflate Mitchell's lungs, squeezing the bag with gradually increasing pressure and watching his little cheeks and neck puff out with each breath that I gave him.

But nothing happened. His little chest did not move and the pulse oximeter reading was very low—only 40 percent when it should have gradually risen to 80 to 90 percent by now. He did have a heart rate—90—but this was also lower than it should have been and ominously, was going down when it should have been going up. Maybe he's already had a pneumothorax, I thought—possibly from my initial efforts to inflate his lungs.

I needed to intubate him so that I could get the bag's inflating pressures directly to his lungs. Normally, I would have given one of the residents a chance to do the procedure, but the intern was too new and the senior resident was getting Michael—now Twin A—ready to move over to the NICU. So I quickly put on my reading glasses and inserted a tube into Mitchell's trachea myself, watching the tip of it slip easily through his miniature vocal cords. The respiratory therapist taped it to his upper lip so that it wouldn't get dislodged, and I began applying pressure directly to his lungs with the bag. And still, nothing happened. I couldn't move his chest, not even a tiny bit. If the resident had put in the tube, I might have assumed that it wasn't in the right place—instead of the trachea, it could have been in the nearby esophagus. But I had put this tube in myself, and I knew it was in the trachea. I applied more pressure, the most I could get out of that bag. And still, nothing.

I glanced at the pulse oximeter. His heart rate was down to 80 now and his oxygenation hadn't improved a bit—it still read 40 percent. If he'd already had a pneumothorax, then the situation was hopeless, and I remembered what I'd told the Chessups. The team looked at me expectantly and I told them no, we're not going to needle his chest. But I suddenly decided to give him some surfactant—a soapy liquid material that we all have in our lungs and that helps keep them partially open at the end of each breath. A premature baby's lungs lack surfactant and so there's a tendency for the lungs to collapse at the end of each breath, making it harder and harder to inflate them with each subsequent breath. The team looked at me quizzically. We always preached that surfactant was not a resuscitative medication. It was normally given to newborn premature babies only after they had been completely stabilized after their birth—nice normal heart rate, adequate oxygenation, and reasonably well-inflated lungs. That was hardly the case here. But the Chessups wanted everything possible done, and while I thought that treating a pneumothorax would be futile and painful, I didn't feel the same about surfactant.

So Jenny, the respiratory therapist, took the small bottle of liquid surfactant out from under her arm where she'd been warming it up, having grabbed it from the refrigerator on her way to the delivery room. I guessed at Mitchell's weight—he was too unstable to put on a scale—and Jenny drew up a dose into a small syringe. Then, through a small side port in his breathing tube, she began squirting surfactant into his lungs while I continued to apply pressure with the bag. Before the surfactant, it felt like I was bagging wet concrete; now, it felt like that concrete had completely hardened.

I turned around and spoke to the intern, who had been intently watching the resuscitation from her vantage point over my shoulder. "Could you bring in the baby's father?" I asked her. "I don't think we're going to make it over to the NICU."

The room somehow seemed quieter after she'd left, even though she hadn't said a word during the resuscitation. The other team had taken Michael to the NICU and there were just three of us left with Mitchell—the nurse, the respiratory therapist, and me. We all stared at the little baby before us, who still hadn't moved or taken a breath, each lost in our own thoughts. I remember thinking, not for the first time in my career, how incredible it was to literally hold a baby's life in my hands, and how depressing it was to realize that there was nothing more I could do. Even though I knew that Mitchell's lung problems were not my fault, I felt like a failure.

And then, there was a subtle change in the bleeps coming from the pulse oximeter, enough to make us all look up simultaneously. The oxygen saturation now read 55 percent and the heart rate 90, and then very slowly, both began to increase—the saturation rose to 60 percent, then 65 percent; the heart rate went up to 95, then 100. By the time Alan walked in with the intern, the baby's oxygen saturation was 80 percent and his heart rate was 110—not exactly normal, but better than it had been. Now I thought we could at least get him to the NICU and see if we could do something more for him with one of our special infant ventilators and perhaps some additional medications.

I was very frank with Alan. "It's as bad as we feared," I told him, as he gazed at his tiny newborn son. "In fact, I called you in here because I thought we were losing him and that it was time for you and Diane to say good-bye. But in the last couple of minutes, he's begun to respond—just a bit—and I think we'll be able to get him to the NICU."

"Is this hurting him?" Alan asked, pointing to the tube taped to his upper lip and the bag, which I was squeezing as hard as I could.

I paused before I told him the truth. "I don't think so. None of the things you're looking at—the breathing tube, the tape, the electrodes—are inherently painful. Probably uncomfortable, but not painful. But since Mitchell can't even cry because of the tube, we'll give him some pain medicine when he's over in the NICU, especially if we decide to do any painful procedures."

"Diane and I do not want Mitchell to suffer," Alan said firmly. "Please talk to us first, just like you said before, if you think he needs to have anything painful done to him."

I assured him that I would keep them both in the loop, and then I spent a moment giving him a much brighter report on his firstborn twin son, Michael.

Alan left the ISR as we prepared to move Mitchell from the

resuscitation table to the warmed transport incubator. I wished that we could make a brief detour into the delivery room so that Diane could see her son, but not only was he too unstable to risk it, Diane was still under general anesthesia—the C-section had to be done so emergently that there wasn't time to put in an epidural.

Jenny had already gone over to the NICU to prepare the special ventilator I'd decided to use on Mitchell. We called it the oscillator, although I liked one of the earlier brand names much better—the Hummingbird. Conventional infant ventilators were typically set to give the baby 30 to 60 breaths per minute, similar to a baby's own breathing rate. The oscillator could be set at rates of up to 900 breaths per minute, more akin to vibrating the lungs as opposed to rhythmically inflating and deflating them. We usually reserved the oscillator for babies who couldn't be ventilated or oxygenated with our more conventional ventilators. In Mitchell's case, I decided to start him on it from the get-go, thinking that the oscillator might be gentler for his smaller-than-normal immature lungs. I also suspected that we wouldn't get anywhere with conventional ventilation since I'd already tried every ventilatory strategy I could think of, using my own hands. And nothing I'd done had really worked—until we'd gotten that little bit of surfactant into him. I was pretty sure that even that wouldn't last for long.

It took only two minutes for the nurse and me to get Mitchell over to the NICU, and that included a brief pause in the hallway so that one set of grandparents could peer at their tiny new grandson through the Plexiglas walls of the incubator. The bedside nurse wanted to weigh him before putting him on his NICU bed because we hadn't been able to weigh him in the delivery room. I hesitated for a moment and then okayed a brief trip to the scale. In the back of my mind, I was thinking that no matter how grim the prognosis, everyone—parents, grandparents, friends, relatives—wants to know two things when a baby is born: Is it a boy or a girl; and

how much did he or she weigh? There wasn't much we could do for
Mitchell, but at least we could weigh him.

His weight was 1050 grams, or 2 pounds 5 ounces. Not bad for
a 28-week preemie twin.

Jenny had the oscillator humming and she quickly connected
Mitchell's breathing tube to it. I looked at his chest from above and
from the side and could not see it shake or vibrate. The respiratory therapist adjusted the amplitude of the oscillations upward and
still, there was no movement of his chest. I had never seen lungs as
stiff as these. The pulse oximeter electrodes were connected to the
bedside monitor and we all stared at the reading—it was back down
to 60 percent. While Jenny continued to adjust the oscillator settings upward, trying to get Mitchell's chest to move and the pulse
oximeter reading to rise, I ordered a chest X-ray and looked around
for the senior resident and intern. They were busy with Michael,
putting in an umbilical vessel catheter to obtain the frequent blood
tests he would need in the first few days of life and to monitor his
blood pressure. When I walked over to his bedside, I could see that
prongs had been placed in his nose, connecting him to CPAP (con-
tinuous positive airway pressure), a quasi-ventilator that supported
each of his own breaths without need for a breathing tube.

"How's this one doing?" I queried the residents.

"Pretty good," replied Gary, the senior resident. "His first X-ray
showed mild lung disease and he's only needing 30 percent oxygen.
We put him on CPAP because he was getting tachypneic and starting to grunt a bit," he explained. This meant that he was breathing
fast. "How's the other one doing?" he asked.

I briefly explained what was going on, tossing in the briefest
of "teaching moments," which included the dire consequences of
not having enough amniotic fluid during critical phases of fetal
lung development. I told them that since they were clearly busy
with Michael, I would go back to Mitchell and put in his umbilical

catheter. Once they were finished, I expected them to join me in managing this critically ill baby so that they could learn something—about both critical care and, most likely, end-of-life care. When I returned to Mitchell's bedside, the nursing staff had an umbilical catheter tray all ready for me. I saw that an X-ray had been taken and was up on the room's digital computer monitor screen. I quickly glanced at it, confirming that his endotracheal tube was in good position and taking in the near "white-out" of his lungs. Air within the lungs should appear dark on an X-ray, and Mitchell's white-looking lungs meant that they were virtually airless. The only relatively positive finding was that there was no pneumothorax—yet.

I put on a sterile gown and gloves and had both an umbilical artery and vein catheter in place in less than five minutes. I sighed, thinking to myself that it was often easier to do these procedures myself, as opposed to teaching or supervising the residents. I'd put in hundreds, perhaps thousands, of these umbilical vessel catheters, but it still gave me a wonderful flush of success when they slid right in and blood came back easily when I drew back on the syringe. Except that Mitchell's blood, which should have been red, was not.

I drew a blood sample and then the nurse hooked the end of the arterial catheter up to a blood pressure transducer. Mitchell's blood pressure was very low, almost too low to measure—another ominous sign. His heart was failing because it was trying so hard to pump blood through the small blood vessels in his lungs.

Almost on automatic pilot now, I started ordering medications, choosing those we typically used for critically ill babies, no matter what their underlying problem. I ordered dopamine, a drug similar to adrenaline, to try and get his blood pressure up; a hefty dose of dexamethasone, a powerful steroid; bicarbonate to try and correct the high level of acid in his blood; powerful broad-spectrum antibiotics in case a bad infection had set in; and morphine, probably more as assurance for me and the staff than for the baby—who still hadn't moved. I'd promised his parents that I'd do my best to make sure he didn't suffer.

Nothing helped. We made numerous adjustments to the oscillator, and periodically I took him off the machine and ventilated him by hand, trying to find something magical that would work. His pulse oximeter reading didn't budge and his heart rate was slowly dropping. I ordered one more chest X-ray, in part to see whether he now had a pneumothorax. It looked no different from his first one. It was time for me to talk to his parents about saying good-bye. There was nothing more we could do for him, I explained to the residents, who were stunned at how poorly he was doing, especially when compared to his twin brother, whose blood was a lovely red color and whose blood pressure was normal.

I walked briskly over to Labor and Delivery, averting my gaze when I passed by the anxious grandparents I'd seen earlier when we'd wheeled Mitchell into the NICU. I knew they were desperate to know what was going on, but information about any baby went to the parents first—and it was up to them to decide what to tell relatives or friends.

The scene in Alan and Diane's postpartum room was fairly typical. Diane had woken up from her general anesthesia but was still groggy, and now nauseous and in need of strong pain relief—she'd had no epidural anesthesia to numb her abdomen. Alan was sitting anxiously by her bedside, holding her free hand in his (the other had an IV in place). An OB nurse bustled about, checking Diane's blood pressure, adjusting the intravenous drip, and administering medications. I stood so that Diane wouldn't need to turn her head to see me and quietly reintroduced myself.

I started with the good news. Michael was a star, doing better than expected for a 28-weeks'-gestation preemie boy. He wasn't needing a ventilator and he had nice, stable vital signs. Then, the bad news.

"We're losing Mitchell," I told them. "His lungs just can't be inflated, no matter what we do, and his oxygen level is very low. It briefly rose after we gave him some surfactant, but that was short-lived. I've tried all sorts of medications, including another dose of surfactant. He's on the best type of ventilator for a baby with his lung problems, and we're just not making any headway."

"Have his lungs ruptured?" Alan asked. "That pneumothorax you told us about?"

"Not yet," I replied, "but I think it's only a matter of time."

Diane closed her eyes, and I wasn't sure how much of what I'd said had been heard by her, or had sunk in. Then, she opened her eyes and looking straight at me, saying quietly, her voice still hoarse from the endotracheal tube, "You're telling us it's hopeless, aren't you?"

"Yes, I am," I said, "or rather, Mitchell is telling us."

Her eyes closed once again and she sighed deeply, wincing at the pain in her abdomen, and quite possibly in her heart. Alan spoke then. "We really don't want him to suffer, so please don't do anything painful just to keep him alive. We'll keep hoping for a miracle…but please tell us when it's time for us to hold him and say good-bye."

I assured them that I would follow their wishes, anticipating that I would be returning to Diane's room within the hour to bring them to the NICU for Mitchell's final moments.

As I walked back into the NICU, into the room where Mitchell lay, surrounded by numerous IV poles containing medications and bags of fluid, by the oscillator and by several beeping monitors, I nearly turned around and walked right back over to L & D to get his parents. The nurses had turned on the audible pulse oximeter alarm and I could hear its low, deep tones — indicative of his very low oxygen level, now down to 30 percent.

He must have had a pneumothorax, I thought. I explained to the staff and the residents gathered around his bedside that I'd talked with the parents and they had agreed that no heroics should be done, including no treatment for a pneumothorax if he developed one. Everyone stood there quietly for a moment. Even if it was the right thing to do—to let a dying baby go—it was still so hard not to intervene.

And then suddenly, a thought occurred to me. Several years ago, there had been a major breakthrough in the care of babies with pulmonary hypertension or "persistent fetal circulation." These were babies like Travis, my transport from hell of many years past, and Harry, whose mother had anorexia and agoraphobia—babies whose lung blood vessels hadn't opened up normally after birth. After years of clinical research seeking a "magic bullet" to help these babies, it was discovered that nitric oxide, a gas normally found in polluted air or "smog," could open up a baby's constricted lung blood vessels, turning them from blue to pink. Once it was confirmed to be both effective and safe, we started using inhaled nitric oxide regularly for full-term babies with severe pulmonary hypertension. It has probably saved hundreds, perhaps thousands, of little lives. Despite its increasingly common use in full-term babies, nitric oxide hadn't been studied in preterm babies, primarily because preemies usually didn't have the same lung blood vessel problems as full-term babies. Recently, though, two large clinical trials had gotten underway to test another use for the inhaled gas—prevention of the chronic lung disease that too often followed the initial preemie lung disease, keeping babies on the ventilator and on oxygen for months or even years. Our NICU was participating in one of those trials and thus our staff had become familiar with using it in preemies. But that use of nitric oxide had a very different rationale from the one I was contemplating now.

Nitric oxide? For Mitchell? How did that idea suddenly come to me, when I'd never used nitric oxide for a baby like him? What made me consider it? It wouldn't hurt him, I reasoned with myself, and I knew that we didn't really understand the reasons why babies without a lot of amniotic fluid around them developed lung problems like Mitchell's. Why not?

I turned to Jenny, who was fiddling with the baby's oscillator dials. "Let's try nitric," I told her. "Twenty parts per million."

She looked at me quizzically at first. Mitchell was too young to be a candidate for the nitric study we were doing. That study recruited babies who were still on a ventilator at one week of age and thus considered to be most likely to develop chronic lung disease. Mitchell was only a few hours old.

"Outside of the study," I explained, in response to her unasked question. "I just want to see if maybe pulmonary hypertension is part of his problem."

She looked doubtful, but we both knew that time was of the essence, so she ran off to get a tank of the gas and the necessary delivery equipment.

Meanwhile, I decided to call Alan and Diane to let them know that we were losing Mitchell, and that it was time to say good-bye. His heart rate was dropping farther and his blood pressure was falling, too.

Jenny wheeled over the nitric tank and the equipment needed to measure its by-products, and hooked it up to Mitchell's ventilator circuit. "Twenty parts per million?" she asked, wanting to confirm my order.

"Yes, let's go for it," I replied. And she turned it on.

The team that was gathered around his bedside paused. All eyes were on the pulse oximeter, which now read 30 percent, and instead of the usual peppy *beep-beep-beep* intoned an ominous deep-toned *hump...hump...hump*, reflecting both his low oxygen saturation and his slow heart rate.

And then, within a minute of starting the nitric, the pulse

oximeter reading began to rise. First, 35 percent...then 40 percent...
and then faster, 60 percent...then 80...85...95...and finally, 100
percent. Even those people across the room, who couldn't see the
pulse oximeter, looked up from their work. They could hear as the
slow *bump...bump...bump* rapidly turned into the much faster *beep-
beep-beep*, matching his rapidly improving heart rate and oxygen
saturation.

A shiver ran through me and the hair on my arms stood on
end. This was one of those moments in my career that I will never
forget: a baby brought back from the brink of death, if only for an
instant.

Alan suddenly appeared by my side, breathless from having run
over from Diane's room. He knew, as he stared at his tiny newborn
son, who was now pink for the first time in his life, that something
miraculous had happened. He grabbed my arm.

"Is he going to make it?" he asked, pleading me with his eyes.

I quickly explained about the nitric oxide, adding that it was
truly an experimental therapy that I had considered at the last minute. And I cautioned that it might not last.

But it did last, and Mitchell never looked back. None of us,
including Alan and Diane, who was wheeled over about 10 minutes
after Alan had run over, could quite believe it. And as I explained
nearly every day on morning rounds with the residents, none of us
understood it either. Why did it work on Mitchell? And why were
his supposedly too-small-to-survive lungs actually performing better than his brother's? Didn't he have fatally small lungs from that
long-standing amniotic fluid leak? Babies like him were just not
supposed to survive.

It took us about a week to wean him off the nitric gas, not
because he showed any signs of needing it that long, but because
we were so afraid that his lung blood vessels would suddenly clamp
down and he'd turn blue again. We held our collective breaths as

we awaited the results of his first head ultrasound, afraid that he'd had a bad brain bleed or a stroke because of his difficult start in life. That would have made me question whether the nitric was really all that miraculous, saving Mitchell only to have his life marred by severe brain damage. But his head ultrasound was normal.

Surprisingly, Mitchell's twin brother qualified for the preemie nitric study. His initial mild lung disease worsened considerably, so much so that by 24 hours of age, he, too, needed a ventilator. Someone commented that maybe it was a case of twin empathy. Twins did tend to do things in a remarkably similar way. In the end, Michael stayed on that ventilator longer than Mitchell did, finally coming off when he was three weeks old. Alan and Diane readily agreed to have him enrolled in the preemie nitric trial—they only wished that they could have chosen to have him on nitric instead of the fake placebo gas, knowing what a miracle it had been for their other son. But as with all clinical research trials, we caregivers would never know whether Michael received nitric oxide or placebo. That's what "randomized, blinded, controlled" trials are all about, and the only way researchers could answer the question about whether nitric oxide prevented chronic lung disease in preterm babies—without serious short- or long-term side effects.

I was off service on the day that Alan and Diane took their babies home, but I'd scheduled the event in my appointment book so that I would remember to go up to the NICU to say good-bye. As I sat in a rocking chair, holding a twin in each of my arms, posing for a farewell picture, I reflected on my chosen medical field. Neonatology had come such a long way in the 25 years since I'd begun my training. I looked down at Mitchell, who was calmly sucking on his pacifier. He was so pink without needing any supplemental oxygen, and I marveled at what had happened. A combination of a new drug, more sophisticated technology, and sheer good luck had saved him.

Two years later I got a Christmas card from Alan and Diane with a picture of the twins on it. They were both wildly rocking on little plastic horses, their mouths open and their hair flying, looking just like any normal two-year-olds. In their letter, Alan and Diane expressed their joy, wonder, fatigue, and gratitude for the lives of their miraculous children. As I looked for a free spot for their picture on my office bulletin board collection, tears came to my eyes. I'd started my collection in 1980, tacking up one taken of me holding Patrick, that incredibly tiny baby I brought over from the delivery room who survived against all odds. In those early years of my career, I took care of so many other babies whose parents never got the chance to send me or anyone else a proud, celebratory photo for a bulletin board. Mitchell could easily have been one of them. Instead, his miraculous survival made me realize I needed a bigger board.

ACKNOWLEDGEMENTS

THESE STORIES HAVE been part of me for a long time; in the case of the first story, thirty years. I didn't want them to be forgotten and so writing them became a perennial New Year's resolution. So many people have helped me fulfill that resolution and I am grateful to them all. First and foremost, I am indebted to my husband, Erik Larson, a gifted writer who read that very first story and later, drafts of the book, and urged me on. Erik introduced me to his long-time editor Betty Prashker who was kind enough to read my first stories. She encouraged me to write more and to put them together in a book. When I was finished, Betty introduced me and my stories to Molly Friedrich, who loved them, believed in them and incredibly, agreed to become my literary agent. Molly made the book a reality by sharing it with Don Fehr, my editor at Kaplan. While other editors had thought that readers might find the book too emotionally draining, Don believed otherwise and made the book's publication a reality. I'm grateful to Kaplan's production editor, Julio Espin, for his heroic efforts to make the book as free of typos and other gaffes as possible.

Several people in addition to Erik were kind enough to read all or portions of the manuscript and provided advice and encouragement for which I am very grateful: Carrie Dolan, David and Sue Woodrum, Michelle McClure, Pete Weigel, Penny Simon, Isabella Knox, Kristee Bingham, Conni Reid, and Peter and Vera Gleason.

Over the years, I was fortunate to have wonderful friends and mentors who supported and coached me in my professional and/or personal life and thus are embedded in some way in my stories: Roberta Ballard, Susan Picone, Richard Martin, David Durand, Abe Rudolph, Doug Jones, Bruder Stapleton, David Woodrum and the late Frank Oski. My parents, Peter and Vera Gleason, have been the bedrock upon which I've built my life and I thank them for being there when I've fallen and cheering me on when I've risen.

None of this—including my ability to practice neonatology while raising a family—would have been possible without the constant support of my husband Erik, to whom I am happily indebted. In addition to his unwavering encouragement of this book, there were so many nights and weekends when I was working at the hospital and he cooked, settled arguments, arranged play-dates, drove all over town, and cheered at numerous sports events. Our daughters, Kristen, Lauren and Erin, have always kept me grounded and shown me what's really important. And our dog, Molly, sat by me for hours as I wrote, waiting and hoping for some delicious crumbs to drop.

Finally, I am indebted to all the babies and their families who challenge us to get it right and to the many dedicated people who staff the NICUs, especially in teaching hospitals where the next generation of neonatal caregivers is being trained. You have all made me realize what an incredible privilege my chosen profession has been.